# a well~crafted home

# a well~crafted home

*Inspiration and 60 Projects for*
*Personalizing Your Space*

## JANET CROWTHER

PHOTOGRAPHS BY JULIA WADE

ILLUSTRATIONS BY TATE OBAYASHI

CLARKSON POTTER/PUBLISHERS

*New York*

FOR DAVIE

Copyright © 2017 by Janet Crowther

All rights reserved.
Published in the United States by Clarkson Potter/Publishers,
an imprint of the Crown Publishing Group,
a division of Penguin Random House LLC, New York.
crownpublishing.com
clarksonpotter.com

CLARKSON POTTER is a trademark and POTTER with colophon is a registered
trademark of Penguin Random House LLC.

Library of Congress Cataloging-in-Publication Data
Names: Crowther, Janet, author.
Title: A well-crafted home / Janet Crowther ; photographs by Julia Wade.
Description: First edition. | New York : Clarkson Potter/Publishers, [2017] |
  Includes bibliographical references and index.
Identifiers: LCCN 2016051052| ISBN 9780553496307 | ISBN 9780553496314
(eISBN)
Subjects: LCSH: Handicraft. | House furnishings.
Classification: LCC TT857 .C76 2017 | DDC 745.5—dc23 LC record available at
https://lccn.loc.gov/2016051052

ISBN 978-0-553-49630-7
Ebook ISBN 978-0-553-49631-4

Printed in China

Interior and cover design by Debbie Glasserman
Illustrations by Tate Obayashi
Cover and interior photography by Julia Wade

10 9 8 7 6 5 4 3 2 1

First Edition

# contents

# introduction

Once you start making things, it's hard to stop. I grew up with a carpenter for a dad. I would sit and watch him in the shop as he cut planks of wood, transforming them into beautiful and functional furnishings. My mom was an avid crafter, baker, and all-around creative mastermind. She taught me the importance of color, texture, and how mixing patterns and styles communicates a vision. I got the best of both worlds with my parents. Construction and aesthetics. Form and function. I didn't know it at the time, but I was soaking in the handcrafting mentality that would later transform my life and my work. Once you realize you have the power to create the items you want to surround yourself with, the possibilities are endless.

When my husband and I moved to New York ten years ago, we had a minimal budget to furnish our apartment. Luckily, the apartment was pretty small. We had to look for ways to save, but we also wanted to ensure that our living space felt like home. DIY projects played a large part and soon our space began to reflect our tastes and style with each new piece we made. We were able to adapt designs to our specific needs and wants, while keeping in mind our different aesthetics. Since then we have moved four times, changed jobs multiple times, acquired one shy pup, and had our first child. Taking a hands-on approach to home furnishing allowed us to be flexible and adapt to every life change while remaining true to our personal style.

This isn't a book about throwing things together you'll end up getting rid of in a few months. Instead, *A Well-Crafted Home* lays the foundation for decorating and DIYing for the long haul. Important pieces that stand the test of time are well designed, practical, and made with good-quality materials. The projects I've featured are easily adaptable and suitable for many environments and tastes. Whether you are ready to tackle a large project or want to begin by homing in on a small detail, you can use this book as an inspirational jumping-off point to building an environment that feels special and authentic. With these techniques and sixty projects, this book will give you the confidence to start looking around you and realize the potential that any space holds. Let's get making!

# the new rules of design

## GETTING STARTED

You don't need to be a design expert to create a beautifully styled home—you simply need a well-curated mix of pieces and an eye for how to arrange them. This book is a guide to help you achieve a pulled-together aesthetic for your home, which looks both deliberate and reflective of your personal style. Can't find that piece you've been searching for? Make it! We are going to go through every room in your home and show you how to turn ordinary materials into beloved home décor. To get started and stay on the right path, let's get organized to plan out the best possible living space.

### Embrace the Mood Board

Mood boards help you flesh out your design goals, find your aesthetic, pinpoint your color preferences, and start to define the direction of your project and space. Begin by pulling images that you love and that truly inspire you. Browse all those magazines and design books you've hoarded through the years or start an online search using sites that allow you to organize your finds, like Pinterest. Collect swatches of textures, colors, furniture arrangements, and patterns you love, and organize them so you have an easily accessible reference throughout your journey. Your board should start to crystallize the style, mood, and theme of the room you will be updating.

### Take Action

Here's how to turn that mood board into a decorating game plan:

- *Identify a feeling.* Do you want your home to feel bright and airy? Dark and moody? Rustic? Refined? Relaxed? As you start to acquire and make objects for your space, remember these words and feelings. I tend to like a little bit of everything. And that's fine, too. You can mix and match your style as long as you keep some grounding pieces throughout your home to tie your vision together.

- *Play with shapes, textures, and patterns.* Incorporating patterns in a room's décor can add personality and keep it from falling flat. Even if you are drawn to a neutral palette, try including quiet tonal colors in patterns of varying scales and styles. Don't be afraid to mix in some fun textures and shapes and a touch of the unexpected—like layered rugs or wallpaper.

- *Find your focal point.* A focal point is the area that demands complete attention when someone enters the room. It could be that gorgeous weaving you just made. Maybe it's your vintage leather couch or that amazing kilim rug you scored at the flea market. Or maybe your home already has some killer built-in features that you can play up, like a gorgeous fireplace mantel or built-in bookcases. Whatever it may be, start to build and design the room around this focal point.

- *Add layers of lavish texture.* Layer pillows on a sofa or sheepskin over your bedding. Place a nubby sisal rug under your area rug. Mix in even the smallest touches of velvet, silk, and wool, and your room will feel instantly more luxurious and pulled together. Don't forget to add some well-placed greenery, which will brighten up any room in your home as well as create a more organic vibe.

- *Make it personal.* Nothing is worse than a home that feels emotionally empty and doesn't echo your sensibilities. The things around you should speak to your passions, tastes, and hobbies so that your space projects meaning and truly communicates your personality and style. Above all, make and collect what you love.

- *Forget the rules.* I'm constantly rearranging my living space. Sometimes you just have to go with the flow and follow your mood. If inspiration strikes, go with it. Your home is ever-evolving because your life is ever-evolving. Adapting your living space to your growing and changing life is a true reflection of you and your family. (If this sounds like you,

furniture on wheels is your friend—I promise!)

> **TIP**
> Once you start a project, you may realize there is a better way of doing it. So craft a plan, but remain flexible as you go. You might just surprise yourself with some off-the-wall ideas that totally transform your space and your DIY projects.

## THE PERFECT COLOR PALETTE

We're not going to get all technical with color theory here because, the thing is, you tend to like what you like as far as color is concerned. A great place to start determining the colors for each room is to use something you love, like a colorful vintage rug or a swatch of patterned fabric. Pull your favorite colors from these objects as the starting point for the hues and complementary colors in your palette.

Paint or tape down your potential color swatches beside each other on a piece of paper. Try to limit the number of colors to three to five per room. Keep in mind that your color palette should flow throughout your home, from the dusty hues in your kitchen to the pops of color layered in your living room. An easy way to accomplish this is to choose one color to ground the whole house and vary the complementary colors in each room. And don't forget about flooring. Take a few potential paint swatches from your local hardware store and throw them on top of your floor to check the tones under your room lighting. Do they go well together and evoke the right mood? This process will help you narrow down the right shades across the board.

If you are color-shy, a good rule of thumb is to keep it neutral (white, cream, beige, *greige* . . . yes, that's a thing!) and then layer on colorful accents with curtains, pillows, rugs, and playful fabrics. This allows you to take it slow and build the room up to the point of color that you like. Small details like brightly colored vases (see page 79), stacks of blue books, the Bleach-Dot Lumbar Pillow (page 45), or different colors of dye samples in the Dyed Fabric Art in Round Mat (page 128) will accent the room nicely.

## SOURCING VINTAGE AND USED PIECES

Sometimes you need to think about what a piece can become, rather than what state it is in currently. You can find beautiful old tabletops that just need a new set of legs, antique linens ready to dye, or vintage picture frames that would become fresh again with a bright coat of spray paint. Make a hunt list, keep an open mind, and get shopping! Throughout this book you'll find several secondhand furniture and accessory projects to inspire you to customize vintage pieces and update them to fit into your home.

## PICKING FABRICS

Many of the tutorials I've provided here call for specific types of fabric. These are just suggestions. I try to specify in the tutorials why each fabric was chosen. Find a fabric that you love and that is durable enough for the project at hand.

To get a sense of the quality, strength, and scale of a fabric, some things have to be touched, so pick out fabrics in person. If you are new to sourcing fabrics or are easily overwhelmed, try going in with a picture and an idea. The sales associates should know where to find what you need and will be able to offer you alternative options. That being said, most online fabric stores now offer swatches. Take the time to order swatches in potential fabrics before buying in bulk. More often than not, once the fabric is cut, you cannot return it.

A fabric choice can enhance or potentially ruin any room or project. Try to consider these three things when making your decision: type of fabric (especially the durability, weave, and texture), quality, and pattern/color. When in doubt, you can't go wrong with high-quality natural fabrics, which will stand the test of time. As a general rule, ask yourself if you are going to love the fabric a year from now. In other words, don't buy a chevron pattern in teal if you don't think you will love it by this time next year. Above all, stay true to your own personal style and ignore what is trending at the moment.

# your diy toolkit

You can always purchase cheap tools and materials before making the commitment to invest in quality. But in my experience, you will save yourself a lot of time, energy, frustration, and money if you initially invest in quality equipment. Buy nice or buy twice. Not only will your final product be superior, but you will also have trustworthy tools to use for years to come. Recognize your ambitions and your budget limits, but also realize that having the right tools for the job makes all the difference in your completed project.

The projects in this book are diverse, but here are the most useful tools to keep around for the majority of home projects. All of them are readily available at your local hardware or craft store; you might even have a few on hand.

## CRAFTING

- Craft glue: E6000, Mod Podge, tacky glue, and spray adhesive
- Craft knife with blade replacements
- Low-tack tape
- Sharp scissors
- Tape measure, ruler, and/or yardstick

## DYEING

- Apron to protect your clothes
- Digital scale, to measure grams and ounces
- Dust mask or respirator
- Plastic buckets and containers of various sizes
- Plastic drop cloths to protect your table surface
- Chemical-resistant gloves
- Eye protection: safety glasses or goggles
- Twine, rubber bands, c-clamps, and clothespins for binding fabric
- Wooden stirring sticks (you can never have enough of these); do not use them afterward for food preparation

## LEATHERWORKING

- 60 mm rotary cutter
- Craft knife
- Round hole punch for leather, in assorted sizes
- Metal-edge ruler or thick-edge quilter's ruler
- Rubber mallet
- Self-healing cutting mat

## PAINTING

- Glass cups for water
- Paint: the most common types include acrylic, watercolor, enamel, and oil paints
- Paintbrushes in various types and sizes

- Painter's palette and/or mixing tray
- Paper towels or cloth rags for cleaning brushes and messes in a hurry

## SEWING

- Bobbins
- Chopsticks for pushing out sewn corners
- Flexible tape measure
- Hand-sewing needles in assorted sizes
- Iron with steam option and ironing board
- Rotary cutter
- Rulers: L-square ruler and quilter's ruler
- Scissors: fabric scissors (I swear by Gingher 8-inch shears) and pinking shears to help prevent frayed edges
- Seam ripper
- Self-healing cutting mat
- Sewing machine: an $80 to $300 machine will provide you with lots of features and accessories
- Straight pins (flat-head pins are good) and safety pins
- Tailor's chalk pencil

- Spools of thread: silk, mercerized, and synthetic

## WOODWORKING

- A sturdy work surface or bench (a garage floor works well, too)
- Bar clamps, set of at least two
- Clamping miter box with handsaw or an electric miter box (the electric version is expensive, at $200 to $600, but worth it if this is going to become a tool you will use frequently; see A Note on Wood Cuts, below)
- Electric drill with bits, as needed
- Hammer
- Level
- Pencil for marking measurements and placement
- Safety glasses, ear plugs, and dust mask
- 12-foot tape measure: Lufkin or Stanley is a trusty, easy-to-read tool
- Vibrating palm sander: a decent one for around $50 will save you a lot of time and sweat
- Wood glue

### A NOTE ON WOOD CUTS

Big-box home improvement stores, like Lowe's and The Home Depot, will perform straight cuts for you. When you buy your wood, make sure to bring exact measurements to save time and money. For the woodworking tutorials, I specify in the supplies lists what you will need cut before beginning the project. Staff at these home improvement stores will not make any angled cuts, like mitered corners. To successfully complete any tutorial with a mitered corner, you will need to purchase one of the saw options specified above.

the entryway

# reclaimed-wood bench

This simple and stylish bench does double duty in looks and practicality. It serves as an easy landing spot for mail, keys, and loose pocket items and fits equally as well at the foot of your bed, stacked high with books and blankets. Move it freely from room to room and see where it feels right for you and your family's needs. The loveliest part about this bench is that it looks like it came with history and a story. To make this project really shine, search for wood boards and lumber with character at reuse and construction salvage stores.

## SUPPLIES

Two 6 x 48-inch wood boards, 1 to 3 inches thick (see Tip)

Five 4-inch zinc-plated mending plates, with 4 holes each

Thirty-two 1-inch Phillips square drive, flat-head, full-thread wood screws #6

Four 18-inch steel hairpin legs

## TOOLS

Tape measure

Pencil

Electric drill

$\frac{7}{64}$-inch drill bit

No. 2 Phillips screwdriver bit

**TIP**

Make sure that both boards are even in thickness. The bench shown here has 2-inch-thick reclaimed oak boards.

**1** Line up the 2 boards side by side, top side down, on a flat work surface. At all times, keep the 2 boards lined up evenly.

**2** Position the first mending plate 1½ inches from the left short edge of the 2 boards. Place the mending plate down and mark with a pencil where the 2 holes need to go on each board. Pick up the mending plate and drill 4 pilot holes (see page 209), making sure not to drill through the board completely. Repeat this on the opposite end of the boards to mirror the mending plate placement.

**3** Place a third mending plate at the center of the 2 boards, mark the hole placement with a pencil, remove the plate, and drill the pilot holes.

**4** The last 2 mending plates will go 8 inches from either side of the center plate. Mark the holes, remove the plate, and drill the pilot holes as before.

**5** Screw the mending plates onto the boards by placing the Phillips screwdriver bit into the drill and, starting with the first plate on the left, screw in all 4 screws to attach the plate to the boards. Attach the rest of the plates with screws.

**6** You can position the legs anywhere you would like, as long as they don't overlap with the mending plates. (I positioned these 3 inches in from the short sides and ½ inch in from the long sides of the boards.) Once you decide where you would like to place the legs, mark the holes, remove the legs, and drill the pilot holes for each leg.

**7** Attach the legs with the remaining screws. Turn it over and you are done!

# dowel wall hooks

Easily hang and simply organize coats, bags, scarves, and hats as soon as you walk in the door. This highly functional bar features the simplicity of round dowels in your favorite solid color. Think outside the entryway with this project—install it under your kitchen cabinets, or along your backsplash to provide easy access to mugs, dish towels, and dried herb bundles. For best results, mount these hooks using the correct screws or hardware, depending on your wall structure and makeup.

**SUPPLIES**

56 x 2 x ¾-inch pine board
Eight 4-inch long × ½-inch-diameter wood dowels
Can of spray paint and primer in one

**TOOLS**

Tape measure
Pencil
Electric drill with ½-inch drill bit
Plastic drop cloth
Wood glue
Sheet of 120-grit sandpaper
Paper towel

**1** Lay the pine board on a flat surface. Line up a tape measure lengthwise and centered on the board, from end to end. Starting at one end, make small pencil marks across the length of the board at the 7-, 13-, 19-, 25-, 31-, 37-, 43-, and 49-inch points, making sure that each pencil mark is centered, widthwise, on the board.

**2** Load your drill with the ½-inch bit. Drill a hole at each pencil mark, going all the way through the board. Try to drill as straight down as possible.

**3** Lay down a plastic drop cloth to protect your surface. Grab the wood glue and put a little wood glue into one hole. Twist a dowel into the hole until it reaches the end of the hole. Repeat with the rest of the dowels. If you are having trouble fitting the dowels, use sandpaper to sand down the edge of the dowel slightly until you can push it through the hole. If any glue seeps out through the top of the hole, wipe it off gently with a paper towel. Let the glue dry overnight.

**4** Once the glue has fully cured, sand down any excess glue on the back so the rack will sit flush against the wall. Also, sand around the top of each dowel for a smooth edge. You can also sand the edges of the pine board to help it look more polished once you paint it. Brush off all the dust.

**5** Spray-paint using a couple light coats of paint over the whole unit. Let it dry between coats.

# woven leather basket

While perhaps not budget-friendly, leather only improves with age and this beautifully handmade basket will develop a wonderful patina over time. The other advantage to making and investing in this project is that it can float to any room in your home: Store magazines beside your sofa, pile pillows into it under the side table in your guest bedroom, keep towels and toilet paper easily accessible in your bathroom, or toss all your winter scarves into it for chic closet storage. This basket goes a long way!

## SUPPLIES

1-inch heavyweight natural cowhide leather strips/
straps, cut to the following lengths:
- four 31-inch pieces (*inside width*)
- three 36-inch pieces (*inside length*)
- three 62-inch pieces (*outside wraparound*)
- two 15-inch pieces (*handles*) (see Tips)

58 large, steel, double-cap rivets, nickel-plated
(see Tips)

## TOOLS

Yardstick or soft tape measure

Pencil

Self-healing cutting mat

Size 4, $^5/_{32}$-inch, round-drive steel
leather punch

Rubber mallet

Rivet setter

Rivet anvil

Scissors

## TIPS

- If you don't want to buy precut leather straps, you can purchase tooling cowhide leather from Tandy Leather that can easily be cut by hand. Turn to page 211 for the tutorial.

- Buy a pack of 100 rivets for cost savings and to have some extras on hand. Not all rivets set cleanly, and occasionally some may need to be reset. Find them at www .tandyleather.com.

**1** All the following marks should be centered, widthwise, on the leather, ½ inch from each edge, down the whole length of the leather strap. Starting with the *inside width* leather strips, working from left to right, pencil a small X at the following inch measurements: ½, 4, 7½, 11, 15½, 20, 23½, 27, 30½.

**2** Next, mark the hole placement for the *inside length* leather strips. Working from left to right, pencil a small X at the following inch measurements: ½, 4, 7½, 11, 15¾, 20¼, 25, 28½, 32, 35½.

**3** Mark all the hole placements for the *outside wrap-around* leather strips. Working from left to right, pencil a small X at the following measurements: ½, 5, 9½, 13½, 18, 22½, 27, 31, 35½, 40, 44, 48½, 53, 57½, 61½.

**4** From the *outside wraparound* strips that we already marked, take only 1 piece and pencil an X at the following inch measurements for attaching the handles: 2¾, 7¼, 33¼, 37¾.

**5** Mark the hole placement for the *handle* strips. Pencil an X ½ inch from both ends, on both pieces of leather.

**6** Place your cutting mat on a flat and sturdy surface. Using the steel punch and a rubber mallet, punch out all the X marks you made, making sure to punch right in the center of the X and checking to make sure that all the X marks are centered on the width of the leather as you go. (This will ensure that the holes line up when you start to rivet the leather strips together.)

**7** To build the basket form, start constructing from the bottom up. The *inside length* strips will sit right at the bottom of the basket. Put them right (or smooth) side down on a large flat surface, spread them about 4½ inches apart from one another. All ends and holes should be in line with one another.

**8** Set the *inside width* strips of leather right side down on top of the *inside length* strips, starting at the fourth hole down from the left ends of the *inside length* strips.

There should now be 12 holes lined up between the *inside length* and the *inside width* strips.

**9** Attach the *inside length* and *inside width* strips together with 12 rivets, where 2 layers of leather overlap with 2 holes lined up. Start at 1 side and move across the grid, pushing the male rivet down through the 2 layers of leather and connecting it to the female side at the bottom. Use the rivet setter, anvil, and rubber mallet to secure the 2 parts of the rivet together, making sure you use the concave side of the setter and anvil.

**10** Once all 12 holes have been riveted together, you can start to form the sides of the basket from the bottom up. Set aside the 1 strip of *outside wraparound* leather that you added the handle holes; this will be the very top and last strap attached. Starting at the second hole of the *outside wraparound* (because the first hole will need to wait to get riveted together with the other end), line it up right under the eighth hole from the left, third hole from the right on the top *inside width* piece of leather. For this whole strip, rivet as you move around the basket, keeping all the *inside strips* on the inside. This *outside wraparound* leather will always stay to the outside of the basket. When you get to the final hole, you will need to rivet 3 pieces of leather together; the *inside length* strip to the 2 ends of the *outside wraparound* strip.

INSIDE LENGTH

INSIDE WIDTH

**11** Repeat in the exact same way with the next *outside wraparound* strip, on the row of holes directly above the strip you just added.

**12** Add the final and top *outside wraparound* strip with the handle holes. Rivet all the holes the same way as you did in step 9, skipping the additional holes you created for the handles as you rivet around the basket.

**13** Rivet the *handle* leather to the inside of the basket with the smooth side of the leather facing out, 1 at a time.

**14** If any strips of leather are a little uneven and poking out from behind the top *outside wraparound* strip, trim them down with scissors.

# soft planter cover

Sometimes moving heavy ceramic planters around your house feels like a chore. This soft and subtle fabric cover slips around your plants in seconds. Use an old plastic planter or the one that comes with the plant at the store as a lightweight and easy option. This cover can be used for a planter up to 12 inches wide. Make sure to drop in a round saucer at the bottom to catch any water drainage and to keep the cover fabric from staining. Go the extra mile and dye this planter using some of the techniques found on pages 197 to 206. Once made, this cover is best hand-washed and reshaped to dry.

## SUPPLIES

1 yard heavy interfacing, cut to 21 x 40 inches

1 yard heavy interfacing, cut into a circle
    that's 13 inches in diameter

1 yard linen or thick plain-weave cotton,
    cut to 21 x 40 inches

1 yard linen or thick plain-weave cotton,
    cut into a circle that's 13 inches in diameter

Thread that coordinates with the linen

## TOOLS

Iron

Straight pins

Sewing machine

1 Iron the interfacing to both matching pieces of linen.

2 Fold over the long piece of linen and pin the short sides together with the interfacing facing out. Sew a ½-inch seam from the top to the bottom and secure with several anchor stitches (see page 207) on each side.

3 Position the circle into the newly created tube with the interfacing exposed and pin at the seam. Pin the circle to the tube in 8 places, with the pins spaced evenly around.

4 Using a short basting stitch, begin stitching at the tube seam, with a ³⁄₁₆-inch seam allowance. Gently guide the fabric underneath the presser foot, easing in the fabric as needed. Once the circle is sewn to the tube, remove from the sewing machine and make sure everything is sewn properly. Return to the machine and restore the stitch length to medium. Sew again around the bottom circle, using a ½-inch seam allowance.

5 Remove the planter cover from the machine and fold down the top edge 3 inches. Turn right side out.

6 Fold about half the tube to the inside (depending on the size of your plant holder). Fold the upper edge over 2 inches to make a cuff.

# block-print pillow

Pillows help soften the entryway and show guests that they have reached a comfortable place. For this project, I chose a vintage, hand-carved, Indian block-printing stamp that showed wear, which came across in the ink variation once I laid the paint down on the pillow. I like this rough and worn look; it gives the fabric a handmade feel. Search for used and vintage block-printing stamps online and at flea markets. Block-printing is an easy way to update an ordinary, solid-color pillow. Don't be too concerned about making a perfect stamping; this technique will add charm by taking on a timeworn look with varied and uneven texture.

## SUPPLIES

18-inch-square pillow insert

Flange-Edge Throw Pillow (see the tutorial on page 47; substitute the chambray linen fabric for a solid color linen and adjust your thread color to match)

Piece of cardboard or thick paper (big enough to fit inside the pillow)

Black fabric paint

Block-printing stamp, any size

## TOOLS

Piece of flat acrylic or flat tray, large enough to roll the brayer over

Brayer rubber roller

**1** Set the pillow insert aside. Grab the Flange-Edge Throw Pillow cover and place a piece of cardboard or paper inside to prevent the paint from seeping through the front to the back side. Lay the pillow cover, front side up, on a flat work surface.

**2** Squirt a dollop of paint directly onto the center of the acrylic sheet. Using a brayer, roll the paint evenly on the sheet until you hear a sticky sound. Then roll the brayer directly onto the stamp until the stamp is evenly covered with the paint.

**3** Turn the stamp over onto your pillow cover and apply even pressure. Lift the stamp up gently while holding the fabric down with one hand. If the block-printing stamp is meant for a repeating pattern, try to place the next stamp down in line with the previous stamped pattern. Repeat stamping as desired.

**4** Once you are done stamping, follow the paint manufacturer's instructions on how to set the paint. Once the paint is completely dry, remove the cardboard and position your pillow insert inside.

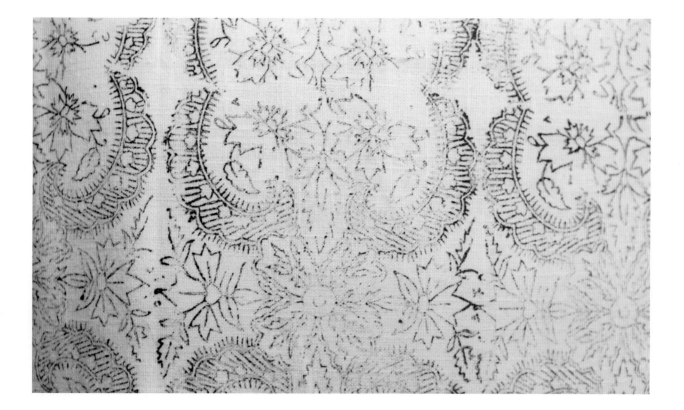

# stencil-brush artwork

Create stunning art for your home with little more than paper, paint, and some imagination. No one would ever guess that you created this masterpiece yourself! With a modern contrast of white and black, this piece really pops, making a notable first impression as soon as people walk in the door. Grab a large open table or a quiet spot on the floor to make this project; it will need a safe place to dry for a couple hours before you frame it.

SUPPLIES

24 x 36-inch watercolor paper

Glass cup with water

Black watercolor paint

Clean shallow cup or bowl

Scrap piece of watercolor paper

24 x 36-inch poster frame

TOOLS

Yardstick

Pencil

¾-inch, flat-head, bristle stencil brush

2 to 3 heavy books or objects (see Tip, page 32)

**1** Lay the watercolor paper, with the 36-inch side facing you, on a clean flat surface. To create a map for the painted dots, mark a 1-inch-square grid over the entire paper using a yardstick and a pencil: Starting at the top left corner, measure ½ inch down from the top edge and ½ inch across from the side edge and mark a dot (this will be your margin). Repeat this on the bottom left corner. Place the yardstick straight across the paper, using the dots to keep it even. After the first dot, mark dots every inch. You should have 24 dots in all, spaced evenly down the width of the paper.

**2** Measure and move the yardstick across an inch. Repeat the exact same marking, creating 24 new dots, 1 inch from the dot before. Continue marking just like this all the way across the paper. You should end up with 24 dots down and 36 dots across, 864 dots total.

**3** Grab your stencil brush and wet it with water, tapping off the excess. Dab the wet brush into the black watercolor paint until the bristle ends are evenly covered. Dab the brush up and down a couple times in the empty cup to remove some of the paint and excess water. Test the stencil brush and paint on a scrap piece of watercolor paper to get the hang of creating evenly painted polka dots.

**4** Paint every pencil mark with the stencil brush: At each pencil mark, dab the stencil brush over it a couple times and squish the brush slightly back and forth to get good coverage. Pull it up quickly and move on to the next pencil mark. You won't need to add more watercolor paint after every dot; I like the look of the dots in varying shades and saturation. When the paint starts to get too light, put the brush back into the watercolor paint and repeat dabbing in the empty cup.

**5** Allow the paint to dry completely, at least 2 to 3 hours, then mount the artwork in a poster frame and hang it on the wall or simply lean it against a wall for a relaxed vibe.

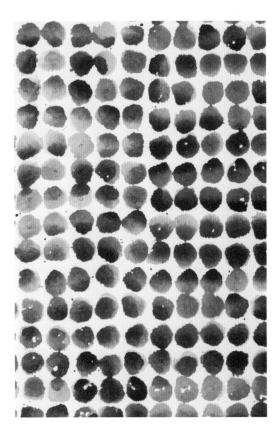

**TIP**
When water and paint are added to the watercolor paper, it tends to warp, which will pool paint in certain areas. Keep this from happening by working in smaller sections and allowing each area to dry in between painting sessions. You can also weight the paper down with heavy books, but be careful not to put them on top of the wet sections of paint.

# looped-tassel wall hanging

Add some texture to your wall without having to learn technical weaving techniques. This large wall hanging will have the same impact. It looks great mingling among frames on your living room gallery wall or hanging above your headboard. Make it in this natural color or liven it up with brightly colored yarn. You could even dip the ends in dye for an ombre effect. Best of all, installation is a cinch: Simply hang it by centering the hoop on a nail.

**SUPPLIES**

800-yard spool 8/4 cotton carpet warp yarn,
    in ivory (www.yarn.com)
12-inch metal macramé hoop
13 x 18-inch metal baking sheet
One 1½-inch brad or picture nail

**TOOLS**

Masking tape
Scissors
Hammer

**1** Tape the yarn to the hoop frame, leaving a 5-inch tail. Begin wrapping the yarn around the frame of the hoop, moving the spool around the hoop in 1 direction. Keep the yarn taut and keep pushing the strands together to create a tight cover around the metal hoop. Cover the entire hoop with yarn until you reach the starting point. Cut the yarn from the spool, leaving a 5-inch tail. Tie the 2 tails together with a triple knot.

**2** Next make the long tassels: Using a baking sheet, tape the end of the yarn on the spool to the center of the baking sheet. Start wrapping the yarn around the length of the baking sheet (the 18-inch side), approximately 75 times.

**3** Cut the yarn off the spool with scissors. Grab 1 side of the yarn loops and pull the bulk off the baking sheet. Cut through the loop in one place, making 75 individual strands of yarn. Lay the bundle on a flat surface. Repeat this step 9 more times, making 10 separate bundles of cut yarn.

**4** Grab one bundle of yarn in the center. Holding one finger at the center, fold the yarn in half over your finger, forming a loop. Don't lose track of the center, keeping your finger in place until you tie the tassel.

**5** Pick up the wrapped hoop at the point where you knotted off the yarn. Center the middle of the loop on one side of the hoop. Pull all the ends of the yarn around the other side of the hoop and push them back through the yarn loop, where your finger is. Pull the ends gently and evenly until the loop tightens around the hoop and all the yarn ends are hanging evenly below. Repeat looping all the bundles around the hoop, side by side.

**6** Gently hammer the nail into the wall. Hang the hoop up with all the tassels centered at the bottom. Using scissors, snip away any stray ends. Embrace the organic nature of the yarn, being careful not to trim too much or you could end up with a much shorter wall hanging.

# the living room

# dyed fabric ottoman

Forgo an ottoman that matches the sofa and make this handcrafted one instead to add style and sophistication to your space. This upholstered stool will become a home for prized picture books, drinks, and possibly a foot or two. Skip the stock fabric and dye your own to complement your color palette and draw eyes to the center of your living space. A simple frame makes this project a doable undertaking even for those with limited woodworking experience. Topped with thick foam, this ottoman will provide years and years of trusty use. When choosing legs, aim to match the height of your other furnishings: The final piece should sit at seat height or a little lower than your sofa.

## SUPPLIES

Your choice of fiber-reactive dye colors (I used 2 tablespoons rust brown, 1 tablespoon rose red, 1 teaspoon orange sherbet, 2 tablespoons indigo blue)

1½ yards of white, linen-blend fabric; try to find 55% linen, 45% cotton (see Tip)

Gentle detergent

4 heavy-duty top plates, with mounting screws included

¾ x 24 x 36-inch piece plywood

Four 12-inch early American wooden table legs, with preinstalled hanger bolt (or shorter for a lower ottoman)

Spray adhesive

24 x 36-inch, high-density foam (I used a thick, 4-inch piece, but anything from 2 to 5 inches will work; the thicker it is, the cushier and loftier the ottoman will be)

45 x 60-inch piece of cotton or polyester quilt batting (buy small rolls to easily accommodate this size)

## TOOLS

Plastic drop cloth

Plastic container

Iron

Electric drill with Phillips screwdriver bit

Tape measure

Scissors

Staple gun with ½-inch staples

**TIP**

I didn't prewash the fabric. Skipping the prewashing step prevents the dye from getting fully absorbed and gives the fabric a bit of a "broken" feeling, with sharper lines and unpredictable absorption. If you decide to prewash the fabric, the dyes will spread more evenly over the fabric surface.

**1** Dye the fabric first. I followed a 2-step dyeing process to separate the warm colors from the cool colors. The first step is to ice-dye the fabric with all the warm colors—rust brown, rose red, and orange sherbet. Follow the process on page 201 for ice-dyeing. Once the excess dye is rinsed from the fabric (don't use soap yet), lay a plastic drop cloth down outside on the grass. Spread out the fabric on top of the drop cloth.

**2** Mix up a 1-gallon batch of fiber-reactive indigo dye in a plastic container (see page 204). Dump the dye all over on top of the fabric, inside the drop cloth. Let it sit like this for at least 8 hours.

**3** Wash the fabric in lukewarm water with gentle detergent and dry on low or hang to dry. Iron to remove the wrinkles. I let my fabric lie out in the sun for a couple days, which sun-bleaches and mutes the colors a bit. (You can always flip the fabric over if it ends up looking too washed out.)

**4** Meanwhile, using the electric drill and bit, screw the heavy-duty top plates to all 4 corners of the plywood board, attaching them at least ½ inch from each edge.

**5** Screw a table leg into each of the top plates, using the attached hanger bolt.

**6** Flip the plywood board so the legs are standing up. Spray a coat of adhesive over the entire top of the plywood. Center the foam on the board and push it down on the adhesive. (Make sure it is truly centered before you press down.)

**7** Place the batting down on a clean, flat work surface. Flip the plywood board and foam over on top of the batting, positioning the batting at the center. You want an even layer of batting covering the top and sides. Cut a 90-degree triangle out of the corners to keep the batting from overlapping at the corners of the ottoman.

**8** Pull the batting taut around the edge of the plywood. Staple a couple times on the underside of the plywood on each side to hold the batting in place. Trim any excess batting. Set the ottoman aside.

**9** Place the dyed fabric on the floor, right side down. Center the ottoman upside down on the fabric. Make sure there is an even amount of fabric around all 4 sides of the ottoman.

**10** Pull the fabric taut at the center of each side and staple the fabric to the board ½ inch in from the edge. Keep stapling and pulling the fabric every inch until you get to about 3 inches from each corner, on all 4 sides.

**11** Now create the corner folds. It doesn't matter which direction you fold the fabric first, as long as you stay consistent on all 4 corners. Pull 1 side of the loose fabric around the plywood corner and tuck it under the other side of the fabric. Staple the pulled side in place, as tightly as possible, to the underside of the plywood. Grab the other loose side of the fabric, fold it down right at the corner, lining up the folded edge with the ottoman's corner edge. You can manipulate the fabric to hide and tuck the excess evenly under the fold. Pull the corner fabric taut to the board and staple it to the underside of the plywood. Add a couple extra staples to this area, making sure the fabric is securely stapled to the plywood. Repeat on all 4 corners.

**12** Trim the excess fabric underneath with scissors, about ½ inch from the staples, all the way around the underside.

**13** To prevent fraying, lift up the edge of the fabric next to the staples and spray a little adhesive between the board and the fabric. Wait for it to become sticky and then press the fabric edges down.

# tassel wall banner

I am always inspired by vintage textiles. A faint stain or a small tear that shows wear is a good thing in my book. When I found this deliciously textured piece of linen stashed in a box of scraps (once used as a simple curtain), I knew I had to bring it back to life. By giving the linen a short splash in a dye bath and then sewing on a few handmade tassels, this project becomes a dreamy work of art, hanging on your wall. You can stick with the calming color palette shown here or kick it up a notch with some bright dye and contrasting thread. The tassels are easy to make but a little time-consuming—best to turn on your favorite movie and get wrapping!

## SUPPLIES

1 yard of linen or plain-weave cotton in ivory, cut to 30 x 28½ inches

1 tablespoon fiber-reactive dye, or package of acid dye in purple (optional)

Spool of cotton thread in natural (or the same color as your linen fabric)

2 x 3-inch piece of thick cardstock

Spool of pink cotton thread

24 x ¼-inch round wooden dowel, stained or painted, if you'd like

30-inch brown suede or leather lacing

One 1½-inch brad or picture nail

## TOOLS

Ruler

Pencil

Scissors or rotary cutter

Straight pins

Sewing machine

Iron

Sewing needle

Hammer

**1** This wall hanging will have 5 sides: top, left side, right side, left diagonal, and right diagonal.

**2** Place the linen right side down on a flat work surface, with the short side facing you. Measure 12 inches up from the bottom right corner of the fabric and lightly mark the raw edge with a pencil. Repeat on the opposite side.

**3** Using the ruler, begin at one of the marks on the vertical edge and angle the ruler until it meets the center of the bottom. Using a very light touch, make a pencil line from point to point.

**4** Repeat on the opposite side. Cut on the 2 pencil lines to make the fabric pointed at the bottom. A rotary cutter makes this task faster and neater.

**5** Make a ½-inch double-fold hem (see page 207) along all the raw edges except the top.

**6** Return the fabric right side down to a flat work surface. Measure 3 inches from the top and fold over the fabric so that wrong sides meet. Crease the fold with your fingers. Fold under ½ inch of the fabric to cover the raw edge.

**7** From the top of the fold, measure 1½ inches down and mark with pins on both edges of the fabric. Sew a ¼-inch seam at the bottom of the fold to capture the raw edge and anchor both beginning and ending stitches.

**8** Sew a seam from one of the pins (1½ inches from the fold) to the other to create a channel for the wooden dowel. Remove the pins. Anchor stitch at the beginning and end of the seam.

**9** If you would like to dip-dye the top, make a small vat of watered-down purple dye. Wet the linen and dip the top into the dye as far as you would like and then pull it out halfway. Let it rest here for a minute. Pull it out halfway again and let it rest for another minute. Pull it completely out of the dye and rinse under cool water. Do not wring. Hang to dry. Press out wrinkles with an iron.

**10** Now make the small tassels to adorn the bottom of the linen. Wrap the natural color thread around the 2-inch width of cardstock until you fill up the whole length. The thread should overlap and be thick. Once you have a good bulk of thread on the card, use scissors to cut the thread off from one side, cutting straight across the bottom of all threads and removing them from the card. Try to keep them as tidy and close together as possible.

**11** From the group of thread, pull apart a pinch full and fold them in half. Cut a piece of pink thread about 10 inches long. Tie a double knot around the natural color threads, close to the top, leaving a 2-inch tail of pink thread on one side. Wrap the long end of the pink thread around the tassel several times. When you get close to the end, bring it back to the start and tie a double knot to the 2-inch tail. Trim the tails close to the tassel.

**12** Repeat steps 10 and 11 to make about 150 to 200 tassels.

**13** To sew the tassels onto the linen, thread a sewing needle with a piece of natural color thread about 22 inches long. Poke the needle up through the back corner of the linen and then back down through the linen, close to your entry point. Pull until you have a 2-inch tail at the back. Knot the 2 ends of thread together to the back of the linen to secure the thread in place.

**14** Bring the needle back up to the front and grab one tassel. Push the needle through the back of the pink threads and then back down through the linen. Pull the thread to attach the tassel, but don't pull too tightly or the linen will start to pucker. Repeat to add the rest of the tassels. I like to go along the left bottom edge first and then start a new thread for the right bottom edge. When the thread starts to get short, tie it off onto the linen and trim the excess. Start a new section of thread just as you did in step 13.

**15** Add as many tassels as you would like. The trick is to start at the bottom of the wall hanging and work your way up, staggering and layering the tassels so the bottom looks lush and full.

**16** Insert the wooden dowel through the top channel. Tie one end of the leather lacing to one side of the dowel, leaving a small tail. Tie the other end of the leather to the opposite end of the dowel, leaving a small tail. Trim any excess leather. Hang on the wall with a simple nail or picture hook.

# bleach-dot lumbar pillow

You would never guess that the pattern on this pillow comes together with household bleach and a couple cotton swabs. The result, which is like something you would find on travels abroad, is inspired by African mudcloth. The indigo color is versatile (like a pair of blue jeans) and keeps the bold color grounded. Make sure to choose natural cotton fabric in a thick plain weave, as the bleach will destroy other types of fabric and will not work on most synthetics.

SUPPLIES

1 yard of 100% plain-weave cotton fabric in blue
    (see Tips), cut to 29 x 55 inches
4 to 6 cotton swabs
Household bleach (see Tips)
Ceramic cup or mug, not used for food
Thread in coordinating color
14 x 26-inch lumbar pillow insert

TOOLS

Plastic drop cloth
Scissors
Safety glasses
Rubber gloves
Yardstick (optional)
Tape measure
Iron
Sewing machine
Straight pins
Sewing needle

TIPS

• You can pick any color fabric you desire but make sure to stick with 100% cotton or a cotton/hemp blend. Synthetic fabrics do not bleach well and other fabrics fall apart after bleaching.

• Bleach a test section first before creating the whole pattern. Each fabric will be different, so test to see how long you need to leave the cotton swab on the fabric for the correct absorption. The bleach will keep spreading once you pick the cotton swab up off the fabric.

**1** Lay down a plastic drop cloth on top of a large flat surface outdoors or in a well-ventilated area. Lay the fabric, right side up, on top of the drop cloth.

**2** Fold a cotton swab in half so that both ends match up evenly.

**3** Wearing your safety glasses and rubber gloves, pour about 6 tablespoons of bleach into a ceramic mug. Dip both ends of 1 cotton swab into the bleach. Touch the soaked ends to the fabric and hold for a little under a second, then move right beside the wet spot you just made and create another, holding down for a little less time than you did for the first spot. Re-dip the cotton swab into the bleach after every 2 spots on the fabric, working all the way down the length of the fabric in a straight line. Repeat this process over the entire piece of fabric. (If desired, you can place a yardstick on the fabric to help guide you.)

**4** Let the bleach dry. Once dry, run the fabric under cool water. Hand-wash with gentle detergent and hang to dry. Press with an iron.

**5** On a flat work surface, position the fabric right side up with the 29-inch side running horizontally. Fold the top of the fabric down to meet the bottom raw edge. The piece will now be 14½ x 27½ inches. Pin the layers together.

**6** Starting at the top right fold, measure vertically 2 inches down and mark this spot. Starting at the bottom right fold measure vertically 2 inches up and mark this spot.

**7** Beginning at the top right side of the pillow (at the fold) and using a 1-inch seam allowance, make a few anchor stitches and sew to the spot just marked.

**8** Beginning at the bottom right side of the pillow at the spot marked and using a 1-inch seam allowance, make a few anchor stitches and sew the raw edges

**9** Reverse direction ½ inch and keep the needle inserted into the fabric. Turn the fabric so that you can sew the bottom seam. Turn again to sew the side, and keep sewing until you have sewn all 3 sides of the pillow. Miter-cut the corners of the pillow to lessen the bulk.

**10** Turn the pillow right side out and smooth the seam allowances. Place the pillow insert through the opening (see How to Pick an Insert, page 48).

**11** Bring the fabric folds of the opening together, making sure they are straight; pin them in place. Hand sew the opening using the backstitch. Knot and snip the tails.

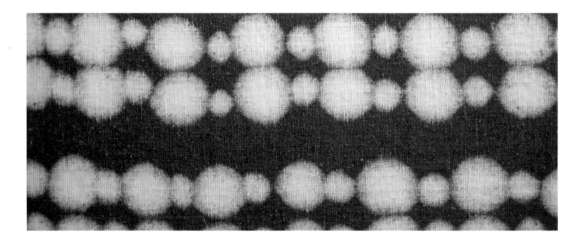

# flange-edge throw pillow

This is the pillow pattern that will stick with you for years to come. Simple, with a little something extra. You can easily jazz up this pillow with a block-printed pattern (see page 27), or by sewing on fun trim or pom-poms around the edge, or dipping the fabric into a dye bath for an ombre effect. My favorite material to use for this pillow is linen, which feels classic and luxurious, but almost any fabric will work!

SUPPLIES

Chambray linen, cut into 3 pieces:
- one 22 x 22-inch piece (*front piece, A*)
- one 22 x 20-inch piece (*large back piece, B*)
- one 22 x 14-inch piece (*small back piece, C*)

Thread in coordinating color

18- or 20-inch-square pillow insert

TOOLS

Sewing machine

Ruler

Iron

Straight pins

Scissors

**1** The vertical edge measurement will always be 22 inches. On 1 vertical edge of the *A piece*, make a zigzag seam so the raw edge won't fray. Repeat for the *B piece*.

**2** Place the *C piece* right side down on a flat work surface. Measure 3 inches from the zigzagged right vertical edge and fold at this point toward the center of the fabric. Iron this fold.

**3** Place the *B piece* right side down on the flat work surface. Measure 7 inches from the zigzagged right vertical edge and fold to the center of the fabric. Iron this fold.

**4** Place the *A piece* right side up on the flat work surface.

**5** Place the *C piece* right side down and match the raw vertical edges on the left with those of the *A piece*. The ironed edge will be toward the center.

**6** Repeat for the *B piece*, matching raw edges on the right vertical side. The ironed edge will be toward the center.

**7** Pin the layers together, taking care to smooth the fabric and pinning closely where the 3 layers overlap.

**8** Using a ½-inch seam allowance, stitch around the pinned pillowcase, beginning and ending with anchor stitches.

**9** Miter-cut the corners, clip the threads, and turn the pillowcase right side out. Smooth out the edges of the seam allowance and straighten the corners.

**10** Make a ¾-inch seam on all 4 sides of the fabric, anchoring the final stitches. This will enclose the raw seams inside the pillow and make a flange edge.

**11** Place the pillow insert into the case, using the open area on the back (see How to Pick an Insert, below).

### HOW TO PICK AN INSERT

Pillow inserts deserve just as much attention as covers. The filling you choose will affect the overall look and feel of the pillow. Do you like your pillows plump and cozy or firm and formed? I personally love a down-and-feather mix, which gives the most comfort while providing a lived-in look that is hard to beat. There are different feather-to-down ratios to consider. It's best to touch and feel what works for you.

Throw pillows and their inserts are measured flat from seam to seam. Once they are filled they become lofted, making them a touch shorter all around. Make sure to keep this in mind if you are going to deviate from the pillow project patterns and measurements in this book.

Tied Shibori Throw Pillow (left), page 52;
Flange-Edge Throw Pillow (center), page 47;
Bleach-Dot Lumbar Pillow (right), page 45.

# tied shibori throw pillow

Made of beautiful shibori-dyed cotton, large in form, with a gorgeously unexpected row of buttonholes and ties at the back, this pillow is simply exquisite. If I dare say so, this might be my favorite project in the whole book! Its understated, casual elegance is so unassuming and utterly consuming all at once. Too much? I don't think so. For a little variation, you can style the ties facing toward or hidden from the room. Make a pair of these for the head chairs at your dining table or prop them up on your bed behind the pillow shams. This throw pillow is definitely worth the effort.

## SUPPLIES

3 yards of plain-weave cotton in a shibori-dyed pattern (see Tip), pressed and then cut into the following 8 pieces:
- one 23½-inch-square piece (*front piece*)
- two 15 x 23½-inch pieces (*back pieces*)
- five 8½ x 2-inch pieces (*tie pieces*)

2½ x 23½-inch piece of iron-on interfacing

Thread in coordinating color

22-inch-square pillow insert

*Note: The fold for the pillow insert runs vertically.*

## TOOLS

Pinking shears

Iron

Ruler

Fabric marker or pencil

Sewing machine

Buttonhole attachment for sewing machine

Straight pins

Scissors

**TIP**
You can find pre-dyed shibori fabric on sites like Etsy. Or, to dye your own loose pattern, lay white or ivory cotton fabric flat on a table and start scrunching it together unevenly from back to front, but staying in a line. Use twine to bind it together in 5 places along the entire length. Throw it into a light blue acid dye for 30 minutes (see page 197 for information on dyeing fabric). Remove the bundle, rinse it under cool water, and then machine-wash and -dry it. Learn other shibori folding techniques on page 206.

**1** Use pinking shears to cut away a small strip of fabric on one *back piece*, along the 23½-inch side, to keep it from fraying.

**2** Place the other *back piece* on a flat surface with the right side down. Place the strip of interfacing, adhesive side down, matching it to the 23½-inch raw edge of the *back piece*. Iron to the fabric.

**3** Fold the interfaced side over so that it is now touching the wrong side of the *back piece*, making the fabric size 12½ x 23½ inches. Press the fold with a hot iron. Place this piece right side up on the work surface.

**4** Find the center of the fabric and then measure ¾ inch toward the center from the fold line and mark with an X, using a fabric marker or a pencil. The buttonholes will run parallel to the fold line.

**5** From the X, measure ⅜ inch to the right and mark a short line to indicate the beginning of the buttonhole. Repeat this to the left of the X to mark the ending for the buttonhole. The completed buttonholes should be ¾ inch long, forming an "I" perpendicular to the marks.

**6** From the center X measure to the right 3¾ inches and mark with an X. Repeat step 5.

**7** Repeat step 6 for the next buttonhole. Returning to the X in the center, measure 3¾ inches to the left and mark with an X. Repeat step 5. Repeat again for the next buttonhole placement.

**8** After all 5 of the buttonholes are marked, lay the fabric on the work surface with the Xs facing up.

**9** Take the piece of pinked fabric and align it parallel with the X'd fabric. Make Xs on the pinked piece for the tie placement. Measure 4 inches from the pinked edge and mark each of the 5 Xs for the ties. Match the newly created Xs with their buttonhole counterparts to make certain the placement is correct.

**10** Place the buttonhole piece right side up with the interfaced edge toward the inside of the machine.

*continues*

**11** With the buttonhole attachment, form all 5 buttonholes, using the beginning and ending at the "I" marks. Clip any threads from the buttonholes and reserve this piece for later.

**12** Now make the ties: Take one of the *tie pieces* of fabric and fold over ½ inch on both short ends. Iron.

**13** Fold the strip in half lengthwise and iron the fold. Fold both lengthwise raw edges underneath the ironed crease so that the strip is now ¼ of its original width. Iron.

**14** Pin from the center out on both sides to secure the strip together, making sure that all the raw ends of the strip are tucked in well. Using a ⅛-inch seam allowance, sew the strip on the 3 open sides, anchoring the first and last stitches. Repeat for the remaining 4 ties to attach.

**15** Find the center of 1 *tie piece* and place this on an X, with the long ends of the *tie piece* running perpendicular to the pinked edge. Pin in place to hold. Repeat for the remaining 4 *tie pieces*.

**16** Attach the ties by sewing a parallel stitch line across the center of the *tie piece*, beginning and ending with a few anchor stitches extending just past the *tie piece* itself.

**17** Return to the work surface and, with right side up, align the buttonholes with the ties to ensure that the placement is correct. Pin these 2 layers together so they don't shift when sewn to the front piece.

**18** Place the *front piece* right side up. Place the joined *back pieces* right side down and match the raw vertical edges with those of the *front piece*. Pin the *front* and *back pieces* together, taking care to smooth the fabric and pin closely where the 3 layers overlap.

**19** Using a ½-inch seam allowance, stitch around the pinned pillowcase—beginning and ending with anchor stitches.

**20** Miter-cut the corners, clip the threads, and turn right side out. Smooth out the edges of the seam allowance and straighten the corners. Place the pillow insert into the case, using the open area on the back (see How to Pick an Insert, page 48).

**21** To knot the ties, place the lower strip halfway into its corresponding buttonhole and pull through. Make an overhand knot and then another overhand knot. Repeat with the remaining 4 ties.

---

## A NOTE ON ACCESSORIES

By displaying decorative accessories like pillows and pretty boxes in smart arrangements and interesting groupings, you let the little stuff create big moments in your home. When arranging groups of accessories, remember that asymmetry is your friend and that it's best to keep things deeply personal. An eclectic mix of handmade items, plus others you have collected throughout your travels, will work well together in telling your story. These items should not be stagnant. Move things around seasonally to keep it fresh and give yourself a good reason to keep collecting. If you're short on space, put out items that are both beautiful on their own and store odds and ends like the remote control and writing implements, such as the Gemstone Box (opposite).

# gemstone box

Add a small whimsical touch to your tabletop, coffee table, or dresser. Then
fill it with jewelry and other knickknacks. Sleek keepsake boxes that hold some
of your treasured things are always good to have on hand. Feature top-notch
gemstones by placing them in minimalist wire settings to adorn the top of
this box.

## SUPPLIES
Can of Rust-Oleum Painter's Touch 2x Ultra Cover
    Paint and Primer in White (see Tip)
Galvanized-steel box with lid, any size you want
Assorted gemstones and crystals
16-ounce spool lead-free, wire solder (3 mm in
    diameter)

## TOOLS
Metal clippers
E6000 glue

## TIP
This spray paint comes in
matte, semigloss, and gloss.
I used semigloss, but the
finish is up to you.

**1** Spray-paint the box and lid with a couple coats to fully cover the steel. Allow to dry for about 2 hours.

**2** Create faux prong settings around the gemstones by bending the wire around the stones with your fingers. Leave some wire showing at the top of the stones and wrap the wire around the back of the stones. Use the clippers to snip off the excess wire at the top of the stones. You can cut the wire at an angle with your clippers and then push the prong closer to the stone. On larger stones, add more than 1 prong setting.

**3** Figure out how you would like to position the stones on top of the box. You can cluster them together or place them randomly on the lid. Wherever the stone hits the box on a flat point, place a small dab of glue on the bottom of the stone and place it on the lid. Repeat for each stone. Allow to dry; glue will cure completely in 48 hours.

# air-dry clay bowl

Organic in form, these bowls break up the solid lines of a traditional bowl. I love the torn edge and, using an unexpected material like air-dry clay achieves this look beautifully. This project is for anyone who is drawn to pottery or ceramics but doesn't have a kiln. Using kitchen nesting bowls as the mold for the clay, you create a lovely set of layered edges when they are stacked on top of one another. Embrace the fingerprints and smudges that come with working in clay. These naturally occurring inconsistencies only enhance the uniqueness and organic, handmade feel of these bowls.

SUPPLIES

2.2-pound package of DAS air-hardening clay

1 cup water, placed into a small bowl

Dish detergent

Gold leaf and/or acrylic or enamel paint
   (optional)

TOOLS

Masking tape

Plastic drop cloth

Rolling pin

Ceramic or metal bowls to use as molds,
   any size you want

Icing spatula

**1** Tape down a layer of plastic drop cloth to a flat table. Remove the clay from the package and tear off about half from the bulk chunk. If you are starting with a small bowl (see Tip), you will not need this much. Wrap up the remaining clay so it doesn't dry out when exposed to air.

**2** Wet your hands and knead the clay for about a minute to warm it up and make it pliable. Place the clay at the center of the plastic drop cloth and press it firmly with your palm. Start rolling it out flat with the rolling pin, working evenly in all directions. Try to keep it the same thickness throughout as you roll. Stop when you get it to about 3 mm thick.

**3** Put a bowl face down on the plastic, near the rolled-out clay. Using your rolling pin, roll the clay very gently around the rolling pin, center it over the bowl, and unroll it to drape it over the top.

**4** Gently push the clay into the shape of the bowl. Use a little water on your hands, as needed, to smooth out any

tiny cracks or uneven surfaces and shape the clay. I kept the edges very organic, but you can rip off sections along the outer edge for different effects.

**5** Let the clay dry for 2 to 4 hours. The thicker the clay, the more time it will need to dry. Before it fully dries, remove the clay from the mold: Gently stick a thin spatula between the mold and the clay and run it around the entire form very slowly so the clay doesn't rip. Once it comes free, set the clay bowl right side up to fully cure, about 24 hours. Rinse your tools under warm water with dish detergent.

**6** You can leave the bowl as is once it's dry, or you can personalize it by painting it with gold leaf and/or acrylic or enamel paint.

**TIP**
**This bowl also looks great on your dining table in a larger shape; see page 101.**

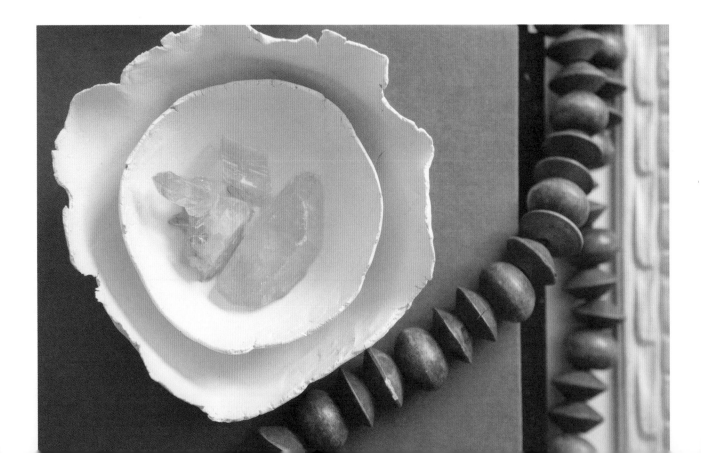

# rolling trunk storage

Trunks help provide the always-elusive "hidden" storage every living room needs. With a can of spray paint and a shiny new set of casters you can transform that purple steamer trunk you bought as a teen or found at a local thrift store. Not only are trunks great for storing items like blankets and pillows, but trunks with flat lids also function as another piece of furniture in the room. Use this trunk at the side of your sofa or as a convenient rolling coffee table.

### SUPPLIES

Steamer trunk

2 cans of white paint and primer spray paint in one

Four 2-inch brass, hooded-plate, ball casters

Twelve #8-32 TPI x 1-inch, round-head,
    combo-drive machine screws

Twelve #8-32 TPI machine screw nut

### TOOLS

Painter's tape (optional)

Plastic drop cloth

Ruler

Pencil

Electric drill with ⅛-inch drill bit

Sheet of 120-grit sandpaper (optional)

**1** Wipe down the outside of the trunk to remove any dirt or debris. If you want to protect the metallic details from paint, mask them with painter's tape.

**2** Lay down a plastic drop cloth outside or in a well-ventilated area. Place the trunk in the middle of the plastic drop cloth. Spray-paint the entire trunk, hardware included, with a light, even coat. Wait for this coat to dry, then spray-paint another layer. Let it dry completely.

**3** Turn the trunk upside down and mark the holes where the casters will be screwed in. You can use a ruler and the plate on the caster as your guide. I placed the casters on the corners, 1½ inches from each edge, but check to see how the trunk was built—you may need to add more space from the edge, depending on the construction of the trunk. You don't want to be drilling any holes through metal.

**4** Drill the caster holes all the way through the bottom. Place the casters on the trunk and screw them on. Turn the trunk over and attach the screw nuts on the inside of the trunk to each screw (see Tip).

**5** Turn the trunk back over. Loosen the spray-painted hardware. You can use a piece of sandpaper to remove tiny amounts of paint around the metal of the trunk for a distressed look.

**TIP**
If your trunk is old and has a flimsy bottom, you may want to add a thin piece of wood inside the trunk for the screws to attach to, for added support.

# framed brushstroke art

Large-scale artwork can completely transform the feeling of a room, and the graphic nature of this painting easily lends itself to any décor. This project can also move from room to room: It works in the entryway, above your credenza in the dining room, hanging horizontally over your bed, or even leaning against the wall atop your mantel. Using a simple, tonal color palette is best here. A handcrafted cedar frame helps make the piece feel special and finished.

**SUPPLIES**

30 x 40-inch stretched canvas

4 ounces white gesso

2 ounces heavy-body acrylic paint in black

2 ounces heavy-body acrylic paint in phthalo blue

8 feet of 1 x 2-inch cedar wood board

**TOOLS**

3-inch flat paintbrush

Flat paint palette

Pencil

Tape measure

Electric miter saw or clamping miter box with
    handsaw

Nail gun with ten 1-inch nails

**1** Using the paintbrush, prime and prepare the canvas with an even layer of gesso. Clean your brush and let the gesso dry fully for 2 to 4 hours.

**2** Create your paint color by mixing the black and blue together on a paint palette to get a very dark indigo color. Add as much black as you would like to the blue paint, but start out slowly, so you come up with the correct ratio before using the entire tube of paint.

**3** Time to paint: Start by making broad strokes back and forth along the length of the canvas. I like to go from one end to the other without picking up the brush to create an even, long layer of paint. Add more paint to the brush as needed. Fill up the entire canvas or until you like the design. Let the paint dry overnight.

**4** To build the cedar frame, cut mitered corners in the cedar board using the saw (see page 210). The cedar will go around the frame with the 1-inch thickness facing out and the 2-inch thickness against the canvas. Make a 45-degree miter cut at one end of the cedar board, cutting into the 2-inch thickness.

**5** Line up the bottom corner of the miter joint to the top left corner of the canvas. The miter cut should extend up. Hold it in place firmly and, using a pencil, mark on the cedar where the start of the opposite bottom corner miter needs to be cut. Use the saw to cut the second miter joint, mirroring the direction of the angle you made for the first cut. Cut another piece of cedar exactly the same way for the opposite side of the canvas.

**6** Start again, cutting a miter right at the end of the cedar. Line up the bottom angle of the miter cut even with the miter cut at the upper left-hand corner (the top) of the canvas. Hold the cedar firmly in place along the edge of the canvas and mark at the opposite (left) side, where the beginning of the miter needs to be cut. Cut the joint. Make sure it lines up correctly on the canvas with the previously cut pieces of cedar and then repeat this size cut again for the bottom of the frame. Now you should have 4 miter-cut pieces of cedar that fit snugly together, forming a frame around your artwork.

**7** To secure the frame, shoot a nail every 5 inches, making sure to shoot a nail into each miter joint.

**8** Place the canvas inside the frame. Line up the front edge of the canvas on one side of the frame. Shoot 2 nails on each side of the frame, going from outside the frame into the canvas.

**9** Hang the art, using a sturdy nail or two on your wall. Place the frame on top of the nails.

# simple diy:
# glass-cover pendant lamp

Using a repurposed glass chandelier shade and a pendant light kit, you can create a beautiful pendant lamp to brighten up a corner of your room. Slide a glass shade over the open cord. Have an electrician wire a socket and plug to the cord. Hang it up by installing a cup hook on the ceiling. Drape the cord down and plug it into the wall socket.

the kitchen

# wooden herb planter

Fresh herbs are surprisingly easy to care for and are far superior to dried herbs. Creating a place to quickly reach for fresh herbs not only enriches the food you are cooking, but it also brightens up your kitchen. This beautiful herb box was made using wood from old cabinet doors we took down in our original kitchen. The wood is simply painted plywood, but I loved the look of the freshly cut boards with painted sides and unpainted edges. Once I sanded the sides, you could see the original yellow color pop through as well (see Tip). I like to keep the herbs in their original plastic planters—they're easier to switch out if one dies or grows large enough to be transferred to the outdoor garden.

## SUPPLIES

½-inch plywood, cut to the following
    measurements:
- two 24 x 6½-inch pieces (*long sides, A*)
- two 5 x 6½-inch pieces (*short sides, B*)
- one 23 x 5-inch piece (*bottom, C*)

Paint and paintbrush (optional)

Two 5½ x 1-inch heavyweight leather straps

4½-inch flat-head screws

Metal or plastic tray to collect water, for inside
    the box

## TOOLS

Pencil

Staple gun with 1-inch staples

Tape measure

Electric drill with ⅛-inch drill bit
    and screwdriver bit

**TIP**

To re-create this rustic look, paint one side of the plywood board and let it dry completely before cutting it to the specified measurements at left. You can also make the entire box and paint it one solid color before adding the leather handles.

**1** Label the boards in pencil on one side to avoid confusion when you're assembling this planter. You can paint the boards prior to assembly or wait and paint the entire planter once it is completed (see Tip, page 67). If you are painting prior to assembly, wait for the paint to dry fully before stapling the boards together.

**2** The bottom of the planter will sit flush inside the 4 sides. Start by stapling the *short side B pieces* to the ends of your *bottom C board* to create the sides of the planter. Make sure the bottom edges are lined up before stapling. Space the staples about 2 inches apart (each side should have 3 staples).

**3** Staple the *long sides A* to the *bottom C* and the *short sides B*. Staple all along the edges that meet the other boards, spacing staples about 2 inches apart.

**4** To add the leather handles, measure and mark a point 1¼ inches in from the edge of the *long sides A* and 2½ inches down from the top edge, on both sides of the box.

**5** Load the drill with the ⅛-inch bit. Drill a small pilot hole (see page 209) at each mark; do not let the drill bit go all the way through the wood.

**6** Take the 2 leather straps and drill a centered hole, ¾ inch from each end.

**7** Line up the 2 holes on 1 strap to the 2 pilot holes on the side of the box. Use a screwdriver bit and join the leather to the box with flat-head screws. Repeat with the second leather strap on the opposite side of the box.

**8** Place the tray inside the planter to collect water drainage.

# rustic footed cutting board

Wooden cutting boards are gentler on knives and much more sustainable than plastic boards. A statement piece, this rustic footed version is crafted from thick, reclaimed wood and sits beautifully atop the kitchen counter. Use it as a daily cutting board or as an occasional serving tray for charcuterie and cheeses. It is substantial in weight but has room for your hands to grip under the board so you can carry it easily to your dining room or coffee table. This cutting board looks best left out all the time.

## SUPPLIES

Three 13 x 7½ x 1-inch oak boards (see Tip)
Four 1 x 1 x 3½-inch square pieces of wood
Four 1 x 1 x 2-inch square pieces of wood

## TOOLS

1 sheet of 150-grit sandpaper
Damp rag
Wood glue
Two 24-inch bar clamps
Paper towel
Vibrating palm sander with
    sanding discs
Tape measure
Pencil
Vegetable oil

## TIP

For this cutting board, you can use any size wood that you find. Just keep in mind that the length and thickness should be the same for all boards and the wood should be thick and sturdy. Some woods, like walnut, maple, cherry, and teak, work better for cutting than others. They are durable and dense, making them practical, heavy-use options. You should never use wood for food preparation if you are unsure about how it has been treated. Old, reclaimed wood from barns, factories, or warehouses looks great but sometimes wood from those sources has been exposed to chemicals and would be toxic to use in the kitchen.

**1** Decide how the 3 boards will fit together. If you can, feature the details on the sides, and put the plain board in the center. Sand down the inside-facing, 13-inch sides of the wood until they are flat and smooth to allow for a better connection. Wipe the sawdust clean with a damp rag.

**2** Apply glue to the 2 sides of the center board and the inside-facing sides of the 2 outer boards. Push them together and slide each one back and forth a bit to evenly distribute the glue.

**3** Place them in 2 bar clamps to let the glue dry overnight. Wipe up any extra glue with a paper towel. You can weight the center board down with something heavy if it pops up as you tighten the clamps. Just make sure whatever you put on top doesn't become glued to the board.

**4** Remove the clamps. Use a vibrating sander to smooth out the top and sides, grinding off any dried glue.

**5** Flip the board over onto the floor. Use a tape measure to mark in pencil where you would like the 4 feet to go: Each foot will be a 90-degree angle, with the edges of the 2-inch and 3½-inch wood pieces glued together. The feet are placed about 1 inch from each edge of the board, in the corners.

**6** Apply glue to each piece, forming the 90-degree angle, and glue them down in place on the bottom board. Carefully turn the board over and add additional weight to the board, if needed. Let the glue dry overnight.

**7** Once the board is fully dry, give it one more pass with a vibrating sander. Dust it off with a wet rag and clean it with soap and water. Let the board dry fully.

**8** To preserve and waterproof the wood, use a rag and apply a thick layer of vegetable oil. Let the oil soak into the board and then wipe off the excess. Repeat as often as necessary. Do not soak the board in water for extended periods or it will crack and warp.

# quilted cushions

Made with lightweight batting and durable cotton, these bright cushions will decorate your kitchen for years to come. The quilting on this cushion is super-easy. I recommend choosing a yarn in a contrasting color for greater definition. You can set these side by side on a Reclaimed Wood Bench (page 15) or add them to the chairs in your dining room. Our dog likes to grab these from the stool and rest his head on them while waiting patiently for another piece of food to drop on the floor.

## SUPPLIES

Sturdy cotton fabric, color of your choosing, cut to
    14 x 32 inches

Thread in color that coordinates with the cotton
    fabric

Low-loft quilt batting, cut to 12 x 12-inch square

Scrap paper

30-inch length of tapestry yarn, color of your
    choosing

## TOOLS

Tape measure

Straight pins

Sewing machine

Scissors

Iron

Fabric marker

2 or 3 safety pins

Large-eye sharp needle

*Note: Supplies listed make 1 cushion.*

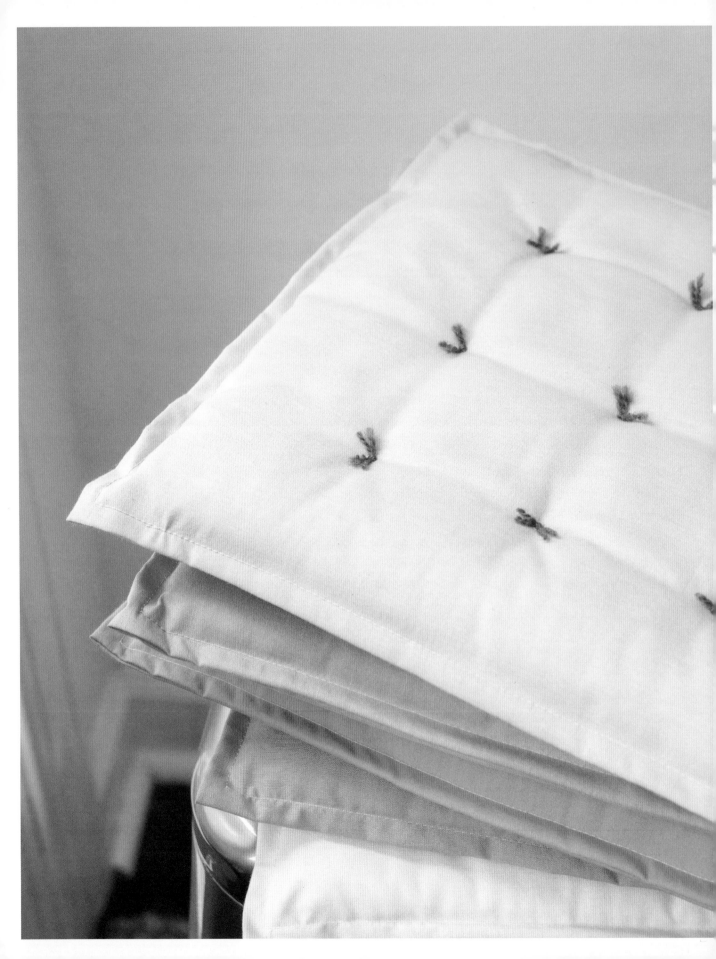

**1** From the fabric, create a square pocket to hold the batting: On a flat work surface, lay the fabric right side up so that the long side is horizontal on your work surface.

**2** Measure 13 inches from the right side and fold the fabric over to expose the wrong side. Fold 1 inch of the raw short edge over onto itself. Pin in place on the top and bottom edges (the length of your fabric will now be 19 inches).

**3** Measure 7 inches from the left side and fold the fabric over. Measure 1 inch from the raw short edge and fold again. Pin in place on the top and bottom edges.

**4** Sew a 1-inch seam along your pinned edges, beginning and ending with a few anchor stitches. At each corner, trim the excess fabric by making a small diagonal cut with scissors, being careful not to cut into the seam.

**5** Turn the pocket inside out so the right sides of the fabric are visible. Smooth out any bulkiness with your hands. Iron the fabric, being careful to press the flap fold straight.

**6** Sew a ⅜-inch seam on all 4 sides of the pillow square to create a flange.

**7** Insert the square batting piece into the fabric pocket. Manipulate it with your hands until the batting is positioned correctly. Smooth out the folded fabric so it lies flat and the fold is straight.

**8** Next, mark the placement for the 9 tapestry yarn ties: Cut a piece of scrap paper into a 3-inch square. Find the center point of the pillow and mark it lightly with the fabric marker. Put one corner of the paper square at the center point, making sure the paper is parallel with the top edge of the pillow. Lightly mark each point with a small dot. Move the paper around all 4 quadrants at the center point so that you mark all 9 points. The dots should be 3 inches apart from one another.

**9** With the back side of the cushion facing up, secure the folded area using 2 or 3 safety pins, pinning the front, the batting, and the backing together.

**10** Cut the tapestry yarn into a 30-inch length. Thread the needle with the yarn—do not knot the yarn. You need to knot each of the 9 dots that are marked, being careful not to tie the yarn to the safety pins.

**11** With the cushion right side up, insert the needle to the right side of 1 mark. Pull the yarn to the back, leaving a short piece at the end of the yarn exposed on the front side. Position the needle at the back so that it will come back through the cushion just to the left of the mark. Carefully pull the yarn from the back to the front. Without removing the needle, knot both strands together with a double knot. Clip the yarn to the desired length of the ties.

**12** Repeat until all 9 markings have been knotted over with the ties. Remove any remaining safety pins.

# leather-loop tea towels

Now that you know about my obsession with linen, you had to guess that I would bring it into the kitchen. Linen's absorbent quality, combined with its antibacterial properties, make it the perfect choice for tea towels. Watch out for linen blends when picking your fabric; you want this linen to be made from 100% flax. This tea towel gets a utilitarian upgrade with a sweet little peek of leather. Use this loop to easily hang the towel from cabinet knobs or the Dowel Wall Hooks (page 19).

## SUPPLIES

3 fabric paints, colors of your choosing
2 pieces 26 x 20-inch prewashed linen fabric, in white and chambray (4 pieces total)
Large piece of cardboard (you can break down a used shipping container)
Thread in coordinating color
¼ x 5-inch leather lacing (see Tip)
Nylon upholstery thread in contrasting color to sew the leather

## TOOLS

3 squirt bottles
Iron
Sewing machine
Scissors

**TIP**
Buy lacing or thin strips already precut or, to cut your own, see page 211. If you have leather that's thicker than ¼ inch, you may need to upgrade to a leather needle.

**1** Fill the 3 squirt bottles halfway, each with a different color fabric paint, then water them down by half. Place the 2 pieces of white linen fabric flat on top of the cardboard outside. Splatter-paint the fabric by squeezing the bottles, one at a time, over the entire piece of fabric.

**2** Layer the colors until you achieve your desired saturation. Let dry. Iron on a high setting to set the paint.

**3** Iron a 1-inch crease on all 4 sides of the fabric with the wrong sides together. The ironed edge represents the edge of the towel at its finished size. Make a double-fold hem on the long side edges, securing it with a ⅛-inch sewing seam.

**4** Repeat step 3 for the short sides of the towel, but this time make sure to enclose the vertical edge seams. Turn the fabric right side up if it's not already.

**5** With the leather strip right side up, place it diagonally across 1 corner about 3 inches down on each side. Beginning about ⅛ inch above the leather lacing, sew 3 anchor stitches into the fabric, not the leather, with your machine. Continue stitching through the leather and sew another 3 anchor stitches below the leather strip, onto the fabric (see Tip). Repeat on the opposite end of the leather lacing.

**6** Pull all the loose threads to the back of the towel and knot the threads in the closest pairs, then snip to neaten.

**7** Wash the tea towel and dry on low heat.

**8** Repeat steps 3 through 7 to make a chambray tea towel without the splatter paint.

**TIP**
When sewing leather, use a long stitch length and go slowly.

# ombré ceramic vase

Bright colors in an ombre pattern come together easily with a couple cans of spray paint, which means the palette possibilities are endless. No flowers? With this statement vase, you'll never miss them. Pick up a blank ceramic vase at your local craft store or big-box store. Look for one with a matte finish, though you can get away with trying this on a glazed surface; just remember to hand-wash it.

SUPPLIES

Old newspapers or a plastic drop cloth

Dark brown acrylic paint

Scrap paper

Blank ceramic vase

Montana gold 400 mL spray paint in 2 different
    tonal colors

TOOLS

Toothbrush

Protective gloves

**1** Protect your work surface with old newspapers or a plastic drop cloth. Mix a tiny bit of water into a tablespoon of brown acrylic paint to make it more fluid. Using a toothbrush, splatter small dots of paint onto the vase: Dip the toothbrush into the paint and lightly tap on a piece of scrap paper to remove any excess that might make an unwanted large splatter. Hold the brush about 4 inches from the vase and comb over the bristles with your finger to send the paint flying. Apply splatter marks over the whole vase. Let the paint dry for an hour.

**2** Working outdoors, put on protective gloves. Open and shake the first can of spray paint. Spray the vase lightly, pointing the opening of the vase away from you as you spray and creating a gradient effect with more paint concentrated at the top of the vase. Don't spray too much in 1 place or you run the risk of the paint running down the vase; a couple of light coats are best.

**3** Open and shake the second can of spray paint. Spray lightly on top of the first color in select spots; again point the opening of the vase away from you as you spray. The key is to create a subtle mix of colors in a couple places but not all over. When you are satisfied with the look you've created, set the vase upright to dry on the drop cloth or newspapers for 2 hours.

# the dining room

# heirloom linen tablecloth

Beautifully offset your patterned napkins and clean white plates by taking a subtler approach to shibori dyeing with this clothespin-created pattern and dark dusty lavender shade. The fringed hem gives this tablecloth a pastoral feel and makes it an enduring classic. It looks best straight out of the dryer, in all its naturally wrinkled glory, draped beautifully over the table's edge. The linen becomes softer and better with use and time, making it a perfect everyday tablecloth.

## SUPPLIES

3 yards of (54-inch-wide) medium-weight linen, prewashed, in white or ivory

4 tablespoons of fiber-reactive dye in color of your choice (I used an equal amount of hydrangea and blue-gray to achieve this dusty lavender shade)

Thread in coordinating color

## TOOLS

Clothespins

Iron

Cutting mat

Quilter's ruler

Rotary cutter

Sewing machine

Scissors

**1** Wet the fabric and squeeze out the excess water. Shake it out to remove any wrinkles. Place the fabric flat on a large, flat work surface, like the floor. Accordion-fold (see page 206) the fabric into 5-inch sections along the entire length.

**2** When you reach the other side of the fabric, fold the left side to the center on the top, then the right side to the center at the bottom, creating a 3-section accordion fold along the width. Using clothespins, bind the edges together along the 2 long edges of the accordion-fold bundle. I used a clothespin about every inch on both sides.

**3** Put the bundle into a vat of fiber-reactive dye (you could also use acid dye; see page 198). Let it sit until you have reached your desired saturation. Remove the bundle and rinse in cool water. Remove the clothespins, then rinse again until the water runs clear. Hang to air-dry or place in a dryer on a low heat setting. Iron the linen.

**4** Using a cutting mat, ruler, and rotary cutter, trim the fabric down to 52 x 106 inches. Exact measurements are not that important, just make sure all 4 sides are cut straight.

**5** Sew a tight running stitch ½ inch from the raw edge, around all 4 sides. If your fabric frayed more as you were dyeing, make sure that you have cut it down enough so that the seam is on a fully woven line and not within the frayed edge. When you reach the starting point, go back and forth a couple times in place to create an anchor stitch to secure the threads. Cut the threads from the machine.

**6** On each side, fray the edge by pulling away the woven fibers parallel to the seam.

# indigo-stripe napkins

I never could keep an all-white napkin in rotation for more than a couple weeks and this deep blue-green pattern prevents heavy use from completely ruining them. Stains just seem to disappear within the lines, making them a breeze to care for. Go a little further and expand your napkin set by overdyeing additional prints and patterns in the same indigo dye bath or opting for a contrasting-color thread to add a personal touch. I chose to use homespun cotton for this project, which is a lightweight fabric, made of fine cotton yarns, woven with traditional techniques. Color variations and small irregularities are typical for this fabric and part of its character and charm.

SUPPLIES

3 yards of striped homespun cotton in indigo
    (see Tip)
Cotton thread in coordinating color

Note: Supplies listed make 4 napkins.

TOOLS

Iron
Scissors
Tape measure
Sewing machine

TIP

You can start with indigo-colored cotton, but why not dye your own? See page 204 for everything you need to know about indigo dye. The base color of my fabric before dyeing was a natural and forest green stripe. The lighter the fabric, the truer the indigo color will be after dyeing. Rinse and wash the fabric a few times after dyeing to keep the color from bleeding during use.

**1** Using a hot iron, press the indigo material, then cut it into 4 pieces that measure 19 x 23 inches each.

**2** Start with 1 piece of fabric, right side down. Turn down 1 side ¼ inch and run the iron over the edge to hold it in place. Fold the same side down another ¼ inch, concealing the raw edge. Give it a press with the iron on the steam setting to set the fold. Repeat on all 4 sides.

**3** With your sewing machine, stitch all the edges in place along the folded hem line. Slow the machine down when you get close to the corners to help feed the fabric through. Snip off loose threads.

**4** Repeat steps 2 and 3 to make the additional 3 napkins.

# clay candlesticks

These faux-ceramic candlesticks are made of air-dry clay, molded around those old brass candlesticks you can find at a thrift store for a few dollars each. I love these simple and elegant hand-molded forms. You can give them a glazed look by applying a coat of nonyellowing clear enamel once the clay is completely dry. Place colorful taper candles in these holders for a playful spin and to break up the all-white look. When these aren't in use on your table, place them on your mantel to add a little drama.

## SUPPLIES
Masking tape
Plastic drop cloth
2.2-pound package of DAS air-dry clay
Water in a small bowl
Brass candlesticks

## TOOLS
Rolling pin

**TIP**
Molding the candlesticks is a very simple process but one that takes patience and a little practice. Don't get discouraged if a hole pops through and you see the brass. This is easily fixed while the clay is still wet. Simply tear off a small piece of clay and coax it into place with a little water.

**1** Tape down a layer of plastic drop cloth on a flat table. Remove the clay from the package and tear off a large handful. You will need about a baseball-size wad of clay for each 6- to 8-inch candlestick. Adjust accordingly if yours is smaller or larger and add more clay or take some away as you go. Wrap up the remaining clay.

**2** Wet your hands and knead the clay for about a minute to warm it up. Place the clay at the center of the plastic and press it down with your palm. Roll it out evenly in all directions with the rolling pin, keeping it the same thickness all the way around. Stop when the clay is 2 to 3 mm thick.

**3** Center the candlestick over the clay. The clay should stretch at least an inch past the top and bottom of the candlestick. Add more clay if needed.

**4** Pick up the edges of the clay very gently. Push the clay around the candlestick, going in one direction until the 2 sides of the clay meet. Coax the clay into all the curves, using water as needed. Once the clay has covered the candlestick all the way around, pull off any excess clay at the meeting point (reserve any scraps). Better to leave a little extra and press it back evenly into the candlestick. Make a loop with your fingers around each curve and twist back and forth, closely conforming the clay covering to the shape of the candlestick underneath (see Tip, page 87).

**5** For the top of the candlestick, gently push the clay over, being very mindful not to rip the clay. Use water on your hands to help prevent this. Coax the clay over the edge and into the hole where the candle will rest. Once the top is even, cut away the extra clay in the hole to allow the candle to fit inside.

**6** Now wrap the clay around the base of the candlestick until it's completely covered (stop at the edge of the candlestick and don't wrap any clay under the bottom). If needed, tear off a rolled-out scrap of clay, and add it back to the base with a little water. Smooth it out to look like a seamless piece of clay.

**7** Go over all the clay one more time with wet hands, very gently smoothing out any lumps, bumps, cracks, or holes. Try to re-create the original curves as closely as possible.

**8** Set the candlestick upright to dry for at least 48 hours before use. Make additional candlesticks if desired.

**9** Be gentle with these clay candlesticks during use and clean them with a wet rag to remove wax and dirt spots, if necessary.

# leather napkin rings

I never had any use for a napkin ring and most of the ones that I see in stores and in traditional place settings have not inspired me to change my thinking. As I was playing with leather cuts and remnants from another project, I started forming rings with notched wings. Instantly I fell in love with the idea of how this type of ring would age with time and use. The added layer of unpolished sophistication these leather napkin rings possess is a thoughtful addition to a modern or rustic table.

## SUPPLIES

4 heavyweight leather strips, cut into 5½ x ¾-inch leather strips (see Tip)

## TOOLS

Cutting mat
¾-inch English point strap end punch
Rubber mallet
Ruler
Pencil
³⁄₃₂-inch round drive leather punch
Craft knife

*Note: Supplies listed make 4 napkins rings.*

**TIP**

Tooling leather works great for this project. Either buy precut strips or hand-cut your own following the instructions on page 211.

**1** Put one 5½-inch strip of leather, right (smooth) side up, on the cutting mat. Line it up horizontally and straight to any line guide on the cutting mat.

**2** Shape the ends of the leather, using the point strap end punch. Place the punch concave side facing the length of the leather, with the center of the convex side lined up at the center edge of the leather. Try to keep the punch as parallel to the leather as possible. The 2 ends of the punch should be flush with the edges of the leather. Punch the edge of the leather with the help of a mallet. You may have to hit the punch several times to get it to go all the way through.

**3** Repeat with the opposite end of the leather. Once both sides are punched, the leather will look like a very long and straight-sided oval.

**4** Measure a ½ inch in from each end of the leather and add a small pencil mark. Center the round hole punch over one of the pencil marks. Punch out the mark with the help of a mallet. Repeat on the other end of the strip, punching out the second pencil mark.

**5** Time to cut the interlocking openings. The thinner your leather, the thinner this cutout will need to be. You want a tight groove so that the leather stays interlocked during use. Start on the right side, lining up the craft knife perpendicular to the length of the strip. At the inner left edge of the round hole you just made, cut a straight line all the way down to the bottom of the strip. Next, move the knife over to the inner right of the hole and cut another line straight down. Remove the line of leather you just cut.

**6** Turn the leather strip 180 degrees so that the cut you just made faces up and away from you. Line up the craft knife perpendicular to the length of the strip, at the inner left edge of the round hole on the right side. Cut a straight line all the way down to the bottom of the strip. Next move the knife over to the right edge of the hole, and cut another line straight down. Remove the line of leather you just cut.

**7** Pick up the leather strip and flip it over to the back. Turn the 2 ends in toward one another, twisting and interlocking the leather ends. If the cuts are too tight, you can keep slicing off a very small amount on 1 side, but don't do too much at once or you'll end up with a loose connection. You can coax the leather into a round shape; with use it will happen naturally over time. Repeat all the steps to make 3 additional napkin rings.

# boro stitched trivet

This charming trivet is made in the tradition of Japanese Boro textiles, where nothing is wasted and scraps of fabric are reused to patch and repair. I collected scraps from various dye projects, but you can easily buy cloth in colors and patterns to match your décor. Reach for natural fabrics, which will resist melting when a hot pot is placed on top. Though the stitch used here is repetitive, once you get going and develop a rhythm, the process will soothe your soul.

## SUPPLIES

8 x 13-inch cotton striped scrap fabric, *A*

8 x 13-inch cotton solid scrap fabric, *B*, for the back

3 x 10¼-inch cotton scrap fabric, *C*

3¼ x 5¼-inch cotton scrap fabric, *D*

Thread in coordinating color

4½-inch length of contrasting trim, ³⁄₁₆-inch wide

3 x 10¼-inch scrap fabric in cotton, wool, or thin fleece (something to give the trivet a little insulation without adding loft), *E*

Cream silk thread

## TOOLS

Tape measure

Pencil

Sewing machine

Straight pins

Iron

Scissors

Sharp needle with eye large enough to accommodate silk thread

**1** Place fabric A right (printed) side up on your work surface with the short edge facing you. From the left long side measure 2⅜ inches in from the edge; lightly mark a seam line down the entire length of the fabric with a pencil.

**2** Place fabric C right side down with the short side facing you. From the long side measure ¼ inch in from the edge; lightly mark a seam line down the entire length of the fabric with a pencil.

**3** Lay fabric C right side down on fabric A and match up the seam lines. Sew along the pencil line. Fold fabric A over fabric C and match up raw edges; pin to hold in place. Both fabric pieces should be right side up with the long ends running vertically.

**4** Fabric D will run horizontally on the long side at the bottom of the trivet. With printed side down and the long edge running horizontally, measure ¼ inch in from the right side, fold over, then iron. Return D to your work surface, right side down, with the ironed edge on the right side, and mark a ¼-inch seam line horizontally on the lower long side.

**5** Now mark the D placement on the layered front piece. Measure from the bottom raw edge up 2¾ inches and mark this, as well as the center of the front piece.

**6** With piece D printed side down, match the pencil line to the marked lines on the front piece and sew a seam on the pencil line. When you sew this seam, it will travel over the folded vertical edge you made with the iron. Stop sewing at the end of the fold so the machine-stitched seam will not be visible from the front. Anchor with 2 stitches and clip the threads.

**7** Return the trivet to your work surface and push fabric D over the seam so all 3 front pieces are printed side up. Smooth the fabric and pin pieces C and D to the raw edges of A.

**8** Mark the center of the front piece on the raw edge.

**9** Fold the trim in half, with the fold pointing toward the bottom of the front piece and the ends meeting the raw edges of the fabric. Place 1 end just to the left of center and the other end just to the right of center, making a gap of about ⅜ inch between the loop. Pin in place.

**10** Place piece E on your work surface. Layer piece A on top with the printed side up. Place piece B printed side down over A, matching the raw edges. Pin the layers together. Secure the loop with several pins from the side you are working on and then remove the pins that are sandwiched in the fabric.

**11** Leaving a 3-inch opening on the vertical edge that has not been enhanced by piece C, sew a ½-inch seam around the trivet. You need to leave a 3-inch opening on this vertical edge so the trivet can be turned inside out after sewing.

**12** Miter-cut the corners and turn inside out, straightening seams and corners. Using a slip stitch, sew the opening closed.

**13** To sew the long silk stitches, thread the sewing needle with a 36-inch piece of silk thread. Knot the end. Sew a long straight running stitch over the entire trivet, going in any direction you would like. As you stitch, be mindful of both sides of the trivet as the stitches will show on the top and bottom. Hide your beginning and ending knots within the seams along the edge.

**14** As 1 piece of thread shortens, tie it off to the inside of a seam and hide the tail within the layers of fabric. Start a new 36-inch piece of thread as needed. When you are finished hand-stitching, knot your thread to the seam, hidden along the edge. Trim the tail with scissors.

# beaded light fixture

Neutral wood beads, paired with a slim pop of color, bring an equal sense of simplicity and charm to a room. Paint a wire basket, used to shape the chandelier, any shade to complement your existing décor. Feeling monochromatic? Paint the beads the same color as well. Try hanging your chandelier over your table (see Tip), just a touch lower than you would think, to add impact and interest to the room. The light diffuses beautifully through the long strands of wood beads. If you live in a rental and aren't able to ceiling-mount this light, purchase an extra-long light cord. You can then screw a removable hook into the ceiling and drape the cord down to plug into an electrical socket.

## SUPPLIES

Can of spray paint, any color you wish

14-inch wire hanging garden basket, chain
    and liner removed

5-inch macramé metal wire ring

28 yards of strong nylon or cotton twine

140 wood barrel white beads, 16 mm x 17 mm,
    with 8 mm hole (look for these at
    www.shipwreckbeads.com)

896 round wood beads, 16 mm (⅝ inch)
    with ⁵⁄₃₂-inch hole (look for these at
    www.craftparts.com)

2 tapped bracket crossbars, 3⅞ inches long
    with ¼ IP tap center hole

Large-screw eye hook with wire nut cover
    to fit back

Thin-gauge steel wire

Light cord kit and lightbulb

## TOOLS

Scissors

Large-eye needle

Wire clippers

**TIP**

If you are going to permanently ceiling-mount this light, consult a professional electrician for the best hardware to match your existing ceiling hardware and wiring.

**1** Spray-paint the wire basket and the wire ring. Cut fourteen 2-yard pieces of twine and lay them flat on a table. Once the wire basket is dry, lay it on the table, with the small opening facing up. Take 1 piece of twine and fold it in half. With the bottom loop of twine, thread it under 1 section of the wire basket, right under the center round ring. Grab the ends of the twine and push them around the bottom ring, then back up through the twine loop. Pull tight to create a loop around the ring with 2 separate 1-yard strands.

**2** Thread 1 white bead over both strands and pull it down to the loop. (From here on out, the 2 strands of twine will remain separate. You can thread a large-eye needle on the twine to help you get the beads on, but you can probably just push them through if needed.)

**3** On 1 of the twine strands, thread 5 round wood beads. Then thread 1 white bead. Lastly, thread 7 more wood beads. Holding the beads on the strand, flip the wire basket over. Push all the beads down as far as you can toward the small ring. Take the twine and pull it up to meet the larger ring (making sure to stay in the same basket section).

**4** Create a secure knot around the large ring with the twine. I like to make at least 2 knots around the wire basket, then bring the longer end of the twine down and knot it one more time around the top of the last wooden bead threaded onto the twine.

**5** With this same piece of twine, thread on more beads in this order: 5 wood, 1 white, 10 wood, 1 white, 5 wood, 1 white. Pull all the beads down, as close as possible to the wire basket. Tie the 5-inch wire ring onto the thread right above the last white bead. Tie at least 2 secure knots around the ring and then bring the twine back down through 2 of the wood beads and tie another knot around and onto itself. Pull the end of the twine through another 2 beads and trim the excess twine with scissors.

**6** Repeat steps 3 to 5, beading the remaining lengths of twine. Make sure to work in the same section on the basket and keep the metal ring and the metal basket lined up. (Be careful not to knot a strand on the wrong side of the ring or the basket won't hang correctly.)

**7** Continue adding more strands of beads in each section on the basket until you have 14 sections in all (with 2 strands per section on the top wire ring). Make sure to loop each new piece of twine in the center of each section. Once you bead the whole basket, you can even out the spacing between each strand. I liked the look of pulling the strands close to each wire section, but it's up to you.

**8** Attach the hardware: Take 1 of the crossbars and remove and discard the green screw. Put 1 crossbar on top of the other and stretch them out to about 5¾ inches long. Two holes should meet up in the center of the crossbars. Put the eye hook down into the centermost hole and cap the screw side with the wire nut.

**9** Place the extended and joined crossbar across the center top of the small wire ring. Wire on the crossbar with the steel wire. Make sure to loop the wire around several times on both sides of the crossbar, making it completely secure. Snip off excess wire with clippers.

**10** Wrap the light cord, socket side inside the beaded light fixture. You can knot the cord to the crossbar or use the eye hook to feed the cord through and knot it.

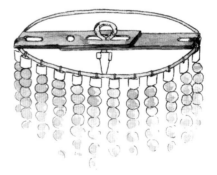

# simple diy:
# oversize air-dry clay bowl

To make this beautiful air-dry clay bowl, follow the instructions
on page 57. This version requires a ceramic bowl, in an oval shape,
to use as the mold. I used a 14 x 8-inch bowl with rippled edges.
To create this oversize bowl, be sure that your clay thickness is at least
3 to 4 mm when rolled out. This will prevent it from cracking
when heavier objects, like fruit, are placed inside.

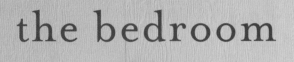

# the bedroom

# linen bedding

My husband and I received a gorgeous linen duvet for our wedding. I loved it to pieces. But, one day, right after we had our daughter, we took it downstairs to our New York City apartment laundry room for a wash. Three months later we realized that we hadn't seen our duvet in a while. Then it dawned on us . . . we never remembered to get it from the laundry room. (If you've had a child, you might understand how this could happen in a new parent's life!) I was devastated and thought there was no way we could splurge on a new one on our budget. I also knew I couldn't possibly go back to a regular cotton bedding set. So, a pattern was born. This is the linen bedding of my dreams—the ultimate in luxury and comfort.

# linen duvet cover

### SUPPLIES

13 yards of prewashed linen (see Tips), 60 inches wide,
    cut as follows:
- sixteen 1¾ x 14-inch strips for ties
- four 106 x 60-inch panels

104 x 94-inch duvet insert (see Tips)

2 yards of satin ribbon 1½ inches wide

Cotton thread in coordinating color (you will need a
    lot of thread for this project, so buy a big spool)

### TOOLS

Iron

Straight pins

Sewing machine

Scissors (and pinking shears,
    optional)

Tape measure

Fabric chalk

### TIPS

• This size will accommodate a bed from full to king. I love using it on my queen-size bed because the sides graze the floor for a romantic and inviting look. I purchased this prewashed linen in white and vat-dyed it this lovely shade of peach using fiber-reactive dye (see page 198). Keep this in mind if you can't find the perfect shade of linen.

• When buying linen, it is best to find it prewashed. If you can't, simply make sure to launder it before beginning a project.

**1** To make the ties, take 1 of the strips of fabric and fold over ¼ inch on both short ends. Iron the folds. Next, fold the strip in half lengthwise and iron that center fold. Fold both long raw edges into the ironed crease so that the strip is now a quarter of its original width. Iron.

**2** Pin from the center out to secure the strip together, making sure that all the raw ends of the strip are tucked in well. Using a 1/16-inch seam allowance, sew the strip on the 3 open sides, anchoring the first and last stitches. Repeat this step for the remaining ties and set aside.

**3** Look at your duvet insert, and identify where the security tabs are located and how many there are. You'll need a piece of ribbon for each tab. Cut the ribbon 6 inches long for each tie. If the ribbon unravels easily, you'll need to cut the ends at an angle or use pinking shears. Set these ties aside.

**4** Join 2 of the linen panels together by sewing a ½-inch seam on the raw edge of the long side. Add the next 2 panels, until all 4 panels are joined together. Sew the first panel to the last panel to form a sack.

**5** Fold the fabric lengthwise at 1 seam to enclose the 2 raw edges. With the bulk of your fabric away from the sewing machine, stitch just to the left of the fold to enclose the raw edges so that they are no longer visible. Repeat on the 3 remaining seams.

**6** Turn the sack inside out. With the seams facing the inside of the sack, fold the tube flat so that there is 1 full panel in the center and the side panels are folded in half, going from the front to the back.

**7** On the front and back panels, position the seams so they are pointing to the center of the sack. Pin the 4 seams just at the top and bottom raw edges.

**8** Sew each seam down flat, sewing close to the left edge of the seam. Reverse the fabric and sew over the seam, getting close to the right edge. Repeat for all seams on the front and back panel. (This will create a flat-fold seam that will hide all the raw edges and extend the duvet's wear during washing and use.)

**9** Optional: Add another flat-fold seam down the middle of the side panels to give it a decorative look.

**10** Place the sack right side up on a flat surface with all the seams matching. Pin at the bottom and make a ½-inch seam. Turn the sack right side in and repeat the stitch at the bottom, enclosing the raw edges.

**11** Place the sack inside out on the bed or floor. Place the duvet insert on top. With fabric chalk, mark the placement for the ribbon ties where the duvet insert security tabs appear. Pin the center of the ribbon at each mark. Sew diagonally across the ribbon to attach and then reverse the stitch and sew again. Repeat for the remaining ribbons.

**12** Turn the sack right side out and make a fold 1½ inches from the top of the entire sack. Iron flat. Take the raw edge of fabric and insert it into the crease. Iron again, if needed. Sew using a ⅝-inch seam allowance.

**13** Return the sack to the bed or floor and align the vertical seams. Divide the middle panel into 3 sections and mark lightly with an X. Find the middle of the side panel and mark lightly at the edge with an X. Pin a tie at each X for 8 total ties. Turn over and position the next 8 ties to correspond with the ties you just pinned.

**14** Attach 1 end of the long strip to the inside of the sack, using the seam allowance as the guide. Beginning at the end of the strip, make a wide zigzag up 1 side of the tie all the way to the top of the seam, then move the fabric over just a bit and reverse-zigzag down to where you began. Use a few straight anchoring stitches. Repeat this for the remaining 15 strips.

**15** Place duvet cover right side in on your bed. Position the insert over the duvet cover and tie the ribbons to the security tabs. Reach inside the duvet and grab the corners with the insert and pull the duvet cover and the insert together so the duvet ends up right side out with the insert tucked inside. Tie the strips together to enclose the insert.

# linen sham

## SUPPLIES

Prewashed linen fabric, cut to the following sizes:

- six 1½ x 13-inch strips for ties
- 24 x 32½ inches, *A*
- 24 x 37 inches, *B*
- 24 x 20½ inches, *C*

Thread in coordinating color

Bed pillow insert; queen-size is best (see Tip)

## TOOLS

Iron

Straight pins

Sewing machine

Tape measure

3 mm double needle

Fabric marker

Scissors

**TIP**

With the help of a secret side flap, under the ties, these shams will hold 3 sizes of pillows: a standard pillow form loosely, a queen pillow form wonderfully, and a king pillow form snugly.

**1** To make the ties, take 1 of the strips of fabric and fold over ¼ inch on both short ends. Iron the folds. Next, fold the strip in half lengthwise and iron that center fold. Fold both long raw edges into the ironed crease so the strip is now a quarter of its original width. Iron.

**2** Pin from the center out to secure the strip together, making sure that all the raw ends of the strip are tucked in well. Using a ¹⁄₁₆-inch seam allowance, sew the strip on the 3 open sides, anchoring the first and last stitches. Repeat this step for the remaining ties and set aside.

**3** Fold over 1 raw edge on the short side of *fabric B* and zigzag over the edge to keep it from fraying, using a small stitch length.

**4** Measure 3½ inches from the zigzagged edge and fold over so wrong sides are together. Iron to hold the crease in place.

**5** Zigzag around all 4 sides of *fabric C*. Now fold over ¼ inch of the zigzagged edge and, using a ⅛-inch seam allowance, sew around all 4 sides.

**6** Sew together the short ends of *fabrics A* and *C* using a ½-inch seam allowance. Lay the piece right side up on your work surface (this will be your front piece). Place *fabric B* (your back piece) right side down on top and match up the raw edges. The front piece will extend beyond the back piece. Pin the layers together.

**7** Begin stitching at the top right-hand side of the back piece, using a 1-inch seam allowance. Continue stitching until you reach the top left-hand side of the back piece, ending with a few anchor stitches.

**8** Because the linen will fray quite a bit when it is dyed, you need to secure the raw edges with a seam. Zigzag around the 3 raw edges of the front piece. Then fold over ½ inch of the zigzagged edge and, using a ¼-inch seam allowance, sew on all 3 sides.

*continues*

**9** Turn the pillowcase right side out and measure 3 inches down from the open back piece. Fold at the 3-inch mark. Now fold over the front piece insert to meet the back piece so both sides have a straight edge. Iron the fold all the way around. At the opening of the sham, use a double needle and sew a seam ½ inch from the fold line.

**10** Turn the pillowcase right sides in and place it on your work surface, front piece facing up. Measure placement for the ties. Find the center of the fabric and then lightly mark with an X just at the seam line, using a fabric marker. This mark will be the placement for the center tie. From the center X, measure to the left 5¼ inches and lightly mark with an X. Repeat on the back piece to mark placement for 3 ties.

**11** Attach the ties. Find the center of 1 tie and place it on an X with the long ends of the tie running perpendicular to the sewn edge. Pin in place to hold. Repeat for the remaining 5 ties.

**12** Attach the ties by sewing a parallel stitch line across the center of each tie, beginning and ending with a few anchor stitches extending just past the tie itself.

**13** Snuggle the pillow into the case. Take the front panel and fold it over the pillow, then tuck the panel inside the opposite side of the case. This will hide your pillow insert. Tie the row of ties into pretty bows.

# linen pillowcase

## SUPPLIES

2 yards of prewashed linen (see Tip), cut to the following
    sizes:
  • 22 x 16 inches, A
  • 22 x 31 inches, B
  • 22 x 31 inches, C
Thread in coordinating color
20 x 28-inch standard-size bed pillow insert

## TOOLS

Tape measure
Iron
Sewing machine
Straight pins
Scissors

TIP

The linen used here was purchased
in a prewashed white and dyed
after sewing, using Alpine blue
fiber-reactive dye (see page 200).

**1** The vertical edge measurement will always be
22 inches. Place *fabric A* right side down on a flat work
surface. Measure from the right vertical edge 13 inches
along the horizontal edge and fold at this point toward the
center. Iron this fold.

**2** Place *fabric B* right side down on a flat work surface.
Measure from the right vertical edge 24 inches and fold at
this point toward the center. Iron this fold.

**3** Topstitch a ¾-inch seam on the folded edge of *fabric
A*. Repeat for *fabric B* and seam the folded edge.

**4** Place *fabric C* right side up on a flat work surface.
With *fabric A* right side down, match the raw edges on
the left with those of *fabric C*. The hemmed edge will
face toward the center. Repeat for *fabric B*, matching raw
edges together with *fabric C* on the right side.

**5** Pin the layers together, taking care to smooth the
fabric and pin closely in the center where the 3 layers
overlap. Using a ½-inch seam allowance, stitch around
the pinned pillowcase, beginning and ending with anchor
stitches.

**6** Miter-cut the corners, clip the threads, and turn the
pillowcase right side out. Smooth out the edges of the
seam allowance and straighten the corners. Place the
pillow insert into the case using the open area in the back.

# framed cane headboard

Tightly ready-woven cane, surrounded by a simple wood frame, will breathe freshness into your bedroom. Whip up this lightweight headboard in a weekend and easily mount it to the wall with screws, or a couple metal brackets. This design is sized for a queen-size mattress. Depending on your existing mattress, you can adjust the length of the top and bottom frame boards to make this headboard shorter or longer. I liked the look of keeping the wood and cane in its natural color. You can easily transform the feeling of this piece with a coat of spray paint or a brush of wood stain.

SUPPLIES

2½ x ¾-inch pine board, cut to the following
   lengths:
   • two 22-inch pieces
   • two 62-inch pieces
6 feet of fine radio-weave cane webbing,
   18 inches wide

TOOLS

Pencil
Electric miter box or clamping miter box
   with handsaw
Wood glue
Nail gun with 1-inch nails
Sheet of 120-grit sandpaper
Staple gun with ½-inch staples
Scissors
Screws or picture hanging hardware

TIP

This project is best done with a
friend. To give the cane webbing
a polished look, have someone
help you keep the cane taut as you
staple it to the wood frame.

1 Lay the boards down on the floor in a rectangle—long pieces at top and bottom, short pieces at the left and right. To build this frame you will need to join 2 boards together to create right angles at the corners. The best way to do this is to cut 45-degree angles at the end of each board, also known as a miter cut (see page 210 for instructions).

2 With a pencil, lightly mark an X at all the bottom corners, at the bottom frame. This will help you remember which part of the board is getting cut off when you miter cut. On each board, miter in a 45-degree cut, making sure to reverse the angle from one end of the board to the other.

3 Once all corners have been cut, join them together. Lay the boards flat on the floor again, lined up as a frame. Work from the top left corner and go clockwise. Place a small amount of wood glue on the inside of the cuts, press the 2 miter-cut boards together, and make sure they are evenly lined up on all outward-facing surfaces.

4 With a nail gun, shoot a nail at the outside edges twice, 1 nail on each side of the miter joints, to hold the frame in place. Continue adding glue and nailing all 4 miter joints. Let the frame dry overnight.

5 Sand down any rough edges or glue that seeped out of the joints. Turn the frame over so that the front of the headboard is facing down. You can protect the wood from getting scratched by adding a blanket or towel under the frame.

6 Line up the cane at the left side. Have a friend help you hold and pull the cane in place. Make sure that the cane will stretch evenly down the entire length of the frame.

7 Once the cane is straight, staple the first edge of cane to the back of the frame, ½ inch from the inner edge, using a staple gun. Add staples to secure the cane about every inch and at least ½ inch from all 4 edges to prevent splintering of the wood. There will be fringe down the length of the cane, past the sewn edge. Leave this fringe to keep the cane from unraveling. Work your way down 1 whole length of the frame. Make sure to keep the cane taut as you go.

8 When you get to the other short end, pull tightly to staple in the final length. Trim off excess cane with scissors, leaving an extra inch of cane webbing past the staples.

9 Mount the headboard to the wall with screws or attach picture hardware to the wall and/or the headboard for easy mounting.

# simple stitch throw pillow

If you are like me and happily drag home hundreds of yards of fabric every time you set foot in a fabric shop (but never really have a plan for its use), then these pillows will become your new best friend. I love finding simple ways to showcase beautiful textiles around the house without much effort. Go crazy because these pillows take only 30 minutes to make!

SUPPLIES

1½ yards of fabric, cut into 3 pieces:
- one 16 x 17-inch piece (*front piece*)
- two 11 x 16-inch pieces (*back pieces*)

Thread in coordinating color

15-inch-square pillow insert

TOOLS

Sewing machine

Straight pins

Scissors

*Note: The opening for the pillow insert runs vertically.*

**1** Begin with 1 of the *back pieces* right side down on a flat work surface. Fold over ½ inch on the long raw edge. Sew the folded piece close to the edge of the fabric with a short stitch length. If the fabric tends to fray, use a zigzag stitch with a short stitch length to secure the folded hem. Repeat on the other *back piece*.

**2** Place the *front piece* right side up on a flat work surface. Add the *small back piece* right side down and match the raw vertical edges on the left with those of the *front piece.* The hemmed edge will be toward the center. Repeat for the *large back piece*, matching raw edges on the right vertical side.

**3** Pin the layers together, taking care to smooth the fabric and pin closely where the 3 layers overlap at the center. Using a ½-inch seam allowance, stitch around the pinned pillowcase, beginning and ending with anchor stitches.

**4** Miter-cut the corners, clip the threads, and turn the pillowcase right side out. Smooth out the edges of the seam allowance and straighten the corners. Place the pillow insert into the case using the opening in the back.

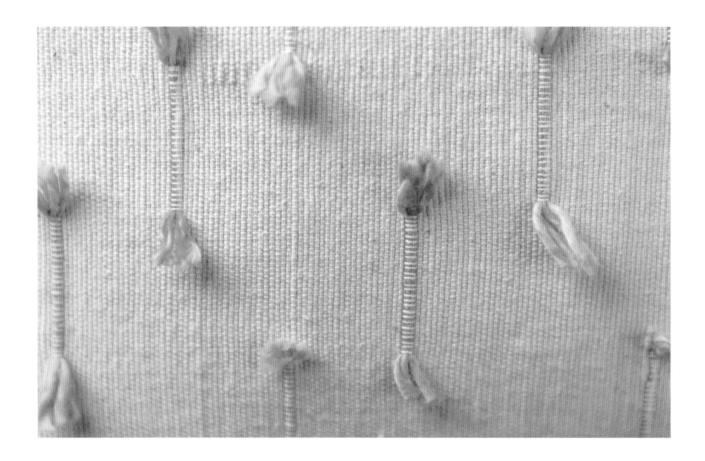

## A NOTE ON THROW PILLOWS

Add a layer of polish to your bed with a tightly curated mix of throw pillows.
Too many pillows will have you loading and unloading them every morning and night,
so stick to 3 to 5 pillows, in addition to the ones you sleep on, for just the right mix.
There is chemistry in the combination: Remember to mix in some color and
pattern to help break up the look of the bed.

# sewn leather pillow

With knife-edge construction, this leather pillow is the ultimate design detail, both carefree and luxe. The wonderful thing about using leather as a sewing material is that you don't have to worry about hems and frayed edges. You just cut it and sew it—simple as that! Don't be intimidated at the thought of working with leather; with a hide this thin and the correct sewing machine attachment, you will have no problem at all. I wouldn't be surprised if you make a whole crop of these pillows once you find out how easy they are. The instructions provided below will teach you how to make a pillow cover for any size insert you have lying around.

## SUPPLIES

Pillow insert, any size of your choosing

Leather hide, approximately 3 to 6 square feet, under 1 mm thickness (see Tip)

Polyester thread in coordinating color

## TOOLS

Tape measure

Pencil

Ruler

Cutting mat

36-inch quilter's ruler

Rotary cutter

Sewing machine

Leather needle for sewing machine

12 small binder clips

Walking foot for sewing machine (optional but helpful)

## TIP

Hides are sold in square feet. You may not need the whole hide for this pillow but buy a large hide and use it to make more than one pillow (see another example on page 14). You need enough leather to wrap around the pillow insert. This thickness (1 mm) is typically referred to as 1 to 2 ounces, as leather is measured by its weight in ounces per square foot. The thinner the hide, the easier it will be to sew and the softer it will be when in use.

1 Using a tape measure, measure the pillow insert by making it as flat as possible or see if the tag is still attached; this will indicate the true size.

2 Determine the sizes of the 3 cut pieces you will need for the *front*, *inner back*, and *outer back*. To get the measurement for the *front piece*, add 1½ inches to the length and width measurements of the pillow form. To get the *inner back* measurement, divide the width of the pillow form size in half and add ¾ inch to the width and 1½ inches to the length. To get the *outer back* measurement, take the *inner back* measurement and add an additional 3 inches to the length.

3 Lay the hide right side down on your cutting mat and figure out the best placement to cut all 3 pieces from your hide. Using a pencil and ruler, draw the lines to be cut for the 3 separate pieces, making sure to keep all angles square. Use the ruler and rotary cutter to cut out all 3 pieces.

4 To sew the pillow, place the *front piece* right side up on your work surface. Lay the *outer back piece* right side down, matching up the top and bottom corners of the left side. This piece will extend across the center but not match up to the right side of the *front piece*. Next, lay down the *inner back piece*, right side down, on top of the existing 2 layers, matching up the right side top and bottom corners. The piece will extend to the center of the pillow and slightly overlap with the *outer back piece*.

5 With a quilter's ruler, measure ¼ inch from all 4 outside edges, marking this line with a pencil. Be careful that the layers don't shift as you mark.

6 Secure the outside edges with binder clips so the leather doesn't shift during sewing. Set the stitch length to 3 mm. Stitch slowly all the way around, directly on the ¼-inch line. Be careful not to dislodge the layers of the leather sandwich as you go, especially where the 3 layers overlap. Remove each binder clip as it approaches the sewing machine foot. When you get all the way back around to your starting point, go past it about 3 mm. Snip the threads from the machine and tie a knot to the starting thread.

7 Trim the corners with an angular cut to reduce some of the selvage edge. Turn the leather cover inside out and push out the corners gently. Insert the pillow form.

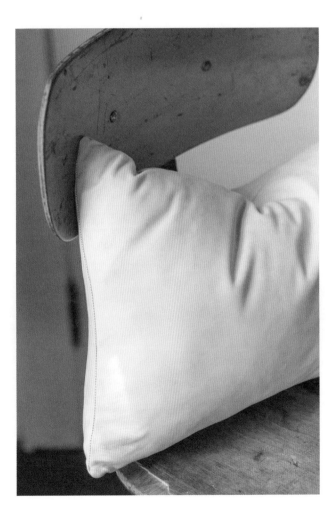

# trimmed waffle-weave blanket

Add a pop of contrasting color and texture right at the foot of your bed to break up its large surface. The waffle weave is inherently cozy, providing warmth without a ton of weight. Beginner sewers: This project is a breeze to make and a perfect project to start you out on that new sewing machine!

### SUPPLIES

Cotton waffle-weave fabric in yellow, cut to
    58 x 60 inches (see Tip)
Thread in coordinating color
Tassel fringe trim in cream, 122 inches, cut in half

### TOOLS

Sewing machine
Tape measure
Straight pins
Scissors

TIP

You can adjust these measurements for any size blanket. Just determine how large you want your blanket to be and add 2 inches to the vertical and horizontal measurements (add 2 inches more if you are going to pre-dye the fabric). Your trim amount will be twice the horizontal measurement of your blanket, plus 2 inches. Before sewing, I dyed white waffle-weave fabric this delicious shade of yellow, using 1 cup of turmeric powder to 1 gallon of water. See page 202 for more natural dyeing techniques and ideas.

**1** Sew a double-fold hem using a 1-inch seam allowance on all 4 sides.

**2** Place the hemmed blanket right side up on a work surface. Measure 1 inch from the end of the fringe and fold over.

**3** Beginning at the top vertical edge of the hemmed fabric, place the folded piece of fringe right side up, with the fringe extending beyond the hemmed edge of the fabric and the header edge of the fringe aligned on top of the fabric's double-fold hem. Pin the fringe to the entire length of the vertical side.

**4** Sew the fringe to the fabric ¼ inch from the interior edge of the decorative trim, beginning with an anchor stitch. Some fringe has a distinctive area where a seam can be added without detracting from the pattern. If so, use that as the stitching guide, rather than the suggested seam placement given here.

**5** Stop 1 inch before you get to the end of the fabric and tuck the fringe back on itself to hide the raw edge. Continue sewing and end with a few anchor stitches.

**6** Repeat steps 2 through 5 to attach the other piece of fringe to the opposite side of the blanket.

**7** Knot any stray threads and trim tails with scissors.

# modern latch-hook stool

Latch-hooking was something I did as a kid and recently this old pastime has started popping up in fun new ways. Create your own distinctive pattern by randomly marking out groups of like colors throughout the white background. While it is faster to buy precut lengths of rug yarn, I like creating an uneven surface by hand-cutting various lengths of yarn, sections at a time. The end result will make the stool cover feel like a handmade, heirloom piece. The basic construction of this stool is easy, but it will take you a couple days to complete the latch-hooking portion of this project. Queue up a few good movies and get started!

## SUPPLIES

3.75 mesh blank rug canvas, 36 x 60-inch package

Three 160-yard skeins of #261 Paternayan yarn, or similar yarn in ivory (see Tip, page 126)

Two 160-yard skeins of #260 Paternayan yarn, or similar yarn in white

Two 8-yard skeins of #325 Paternayan yarn, or similar yarn in light plum

One 8-yard skein of #886 Paternayan yarn, or similar yarn in light peach

Two 8-yard skeins of neon yellow Paternayan yarn, or similar yarn in yellow

5 yards of #3 or #4 sage green wool yarn

5 yards of #3 or #4 fire-red wool yarn

8 yards of #6 or #7 rust-color thick wool roving yarn

Four 16-inch Wegner Danish modern leg, in soft maple (Home Depot or Lowe's)

15-inch edge-glued pine round, 1 inch thick (Home Depot or Lowe's)

Four Waddell angle top table leg installation plates (Home Depot or Lowe's)

Sixteen 1-inch screws to fit mounting plate holes

Wood stain with soft cloth and rubber gloves (optional)

## TOOLS

Permanent marker

Protractor

Scissors

¼-inch latch hook

Pencil

Electric drill with screwdriver attachment

Staple gun with ½-inch staples

TIP

I used Paternayan yarn for this project because I love the texture and colors of these yarns. The yarn splits into 3 separate strands, which gives this stool a very lush and full texture once completed. However, this means that the yarn is a little trickier to work with than traditional yarns. Paternayan brand yarn is also pricier than most store-bought yarns. To cut down on costs, you can easily switch to another brand. Almost anything will work, but try to stick with more natural fibers because some yarns made of synthetics will have a sheen at the cut edge, making your finished piece feel a little cheaper in quality. Pick up yarn in the #3 to #6 weight range for best results.

**1** With a permanent marker and a protractor, draw an 18-inch circle on the rug canvas. Cut out the circle, leaving roughly a 2-inch border. You should end up with a rough-cut 22-inch circle, with the 18-inch circle marked clearly on the inside.

**2** Start cutting 3- to 4-inch sections of yarn with scissors. Keep each color bundled together. Since Paternayan yarn comes in long sections, I like to unravel the main skein and cut sections into the bulk lengths of the yarn. Cutting many strands at once makes this process a lot faster. Don't worry too much about measuring each cut. You don't need to cut all the yarn, just enough to get you started. You can cut more as you go.

**3** To use the latch hook, try a couple tests along the outer edge of the canvas. Grab a piece of yarn and fold it in half. Push the latch hook through the loop of the yarn. Now push the latch hook down through the center of 1 grid square on the canvas and then back up through the next grid square on the canvas. The latch-hook lever should be open. Take the ends of the yarn and pull them up together, wrapping them over the lever and into the open mouth of the hook.

**4** Pull the tool downward (toward you), back though the 2 canvas grids. The latch should snap up, enclosing the yarn inside the hook as you pull. Let go of the yarn with your fingers and pull the latch hook all the way back through the canvas. This motion will loop the yarn around the canvas. Pull on the ends to tighten and elongate the yarn. Once you pick up speed, the tool will do most of the tightening for you. You can latch down the grid vertically, horizontally, or anyway you like—whatever feels most comfortable to you.

**5** Start by creating the areas of color first. Hook the color yarn to the canvas anywhere you like, but make sure to keep all yarn inside the 18-inch circle. The design is completely up to you and can be predetermined or you can wing it as you move along the canvas.

**6** Once all the color is looped to your liking, add the white and ivory yarn. I cut off several lengths of yarn in both colors and mixed them randomly as I latched the yarn to the canvas. It is a very subtle color change, but this gives the large white space some added depth and dimension.

**7** Once you fill in the entire 18-inch circle with yarn, it is time to put together the stool. Attach the legs to the round base first and then add the looped canvas. Find the center of the round board and draw a cross with a pencil, determining the north, south, east, and west.

**8** Screw 1 leg into the center of each mounting plate. Using the drill and screws, drill in all 4 mounting plates, 1 on each drawn line, 1 inch from the outer edge of the round board.

**9** Stain or paint the legs, if desired. I gave each of my legs a wash of peach stain. Wait for this to dry before attaching the legs to the hooked canvas.

**10** Lay the hooked canvas, loft side down, on the floor. Turn the stool over and place the round board at the center of the latched canvas.

**11** To attach the latched canvas to the pine board, use a staple gun. Pull the north side of the canvas up and over the edge of the board, then staple it to the back. Move to the south side and pull it up over the edge, then staple in place. Repeat on the east and west side. Keep moving around the canvas, mirroring your position after each staple. Staple about every 2 inches around the whole board. You will have bubbles of canvas arched up between the staples. Use the staple gun to go over these and smooth them down in place.

# dyed fabric art in round mat

I was searching for a way to showcase the scrap pieces of fabric I'd accumulated while dyeing test swatches. Dyed fabric on its own can be so beautiful that it deserves its moment in the spotlight. Pairing the fabric with a custom-cut, framed, round mat is the perfect solution. Group a few frames together to make a real statement. Once you see how easy it is to cut round mats, you'll find plenty of excuses to create more round matted portraits for other rooms in your home as well. The custom mat will make the object or image inside feel special and distinctive.

SUPPLIES

12-inch-square picture frame
20 x 32-inch matboard in white
Dyed fabric swatch, at least 8 inches square

TOOLS

Pencil
Cutting mat
Ruler
Rotary cutter
Heavy-duty circle cutter (Olfa is my favorite brand, but there are lots of options on the market)
Archival double-sided tape

**1** Remove the back chipboard from the frame. Using it as a guide to cut the square into the matboard, place the chipboard down on top of the matboard and mark a light pencil line along all four edges.

**2** Place the matboard on a cutting mat. Use a ruler and place it right to the inside of your marked line; cut out all 4 lines with a rotary cutter.

**3** Turn the matboard over, right side down. Using a ruler, draw a straight line between the top left corner and the bottom right corner. Do the same in the reverse direction, drawing a straight line from the top right corner to the bottom left corner. The point at which the lines meet is the center of the matboard.

**4** Line up the circle cutter to cut an 8-inch circle, which means the blade will be 4 inches away from the center point. Push the point of the circle cutter down at the center of the matboard. Push down firmly and swing the blade all the way around, while holding the matboard in place, cutting the 8-inch circle out from the matboard.

**5** Mount the fabric on the chipboard with double-sided tape. It is better not to tape the fabric directly to the matboard because you may want to change out the pattern or reuse the matboard later.

**6** Place the matboard, right side toward the glass, then put the chipboard, with fabric attached, back in the frame and secure with the clips (or hooks) on the back.

# natural jute rug

Inspired by Scandinavian design, this rug is a grounding force right next to your bed. I adore this rug with its easygoing vibe, earth-tone shades, and rich texture. I've seen similar DIYs for this type of rug before, but all of them call for a hot-glue gun and a lot of patience. I don't like the thought of using a hot-glue gun on something that is going to get repeated use, as it generally does not stand the test of time. After a few attempts I came up with this method, utilizing painter's tape, fabric glue, and some fabric for reinforcement and long-term durability. I think you'll like the streamlined process. This rug can be created using the same technique in many shapes and sizes. Try a long runner or a small entryway mat. Make this work for you!

SUPPLIES

Approximately 1,000 feet of 4-ply jute twine
(see Tip)

1½ yards of duck fabric (7–10 ounces is best; make
sure the width is more than 48 inches) or a
canvas drop cloth

8 ounces of Mod Podge matte glue

TOOLS

A large table or available flat floor surface

Painter's tape

Tape measure

Scissors

Mini paint roller or large sponge

TIP

You can make this rug any size to fit your space by subtracting or adding more jute twine as well as enough fabric to cover the bottom. Uline.com sells an inexpensive large spool of 3,700 feet. I suggest buying this if you plan to make a larger rug or additional rugs.

1 Choose a large flat area to build the rug, like a dining room table or a low-traffic spot on the floor. The rug will need to stay in one place through the whole tutorial, and it has to dry overnight.

2 Tear off 5 sections of painter's tape, each about 5 inches long. Stick the edges parallel to one another, overlapping about 2 to 3 mm to form a square of tape. Lay the sticky side up on your flat working surface.

3 Grab the jute twine, and pinch the end back onto itself to start a tight coil. Roll the twine around the start a couple times until you have a circle about an inch in diameter. Press the circle firmly and flat to the center of the tape square. The tape will hold it in place.

4 I like to work from a larger spool of twine and pull from the top center. This elevates the twine while you work, which helps keep the twine from sticking to the tape until you press it into place. This also helps the project go a lot faster, as the twine will not tangle as you go. Use both hands, 1 to rotate the coil and 1 to add more jute twine around the outer edge. As you go, press each section of twine firmly onto the tape. You will start to develop a rhythm and figure out the most comfortable way to work.

5 As soon as any section of the coil has reached the edges of the tape, tear off more sections of tape and add them under the previous sections, extending the sticky surface area. Repeat as needed. Eventually, the whole back of the rug will be covered in tape.

6 Keep coiling the jute twine tightly; you don't want any gaps between the rows. The coil will start to warp a little bit as you reach about an 8- to 12-inch diameter. But as you keep adding width to the rug, it will settle down and become flat again.

7 Keep coiling the jute until the rug reaches 4 feet in diameter. Cut the end of the twine at a slight angle and tuck it right into the side of the rug.

8 Place the duck fabric on top of the coil, making sure every part is covered by fabric. Pull up half the fabric and fold it onto itself, exposing half the coiled twine below. We are going to glue half the rug first because the glue dries quickly when exposed to air. Squirt a generous amount of glue all over the exposed coil (not too much, though, or you risk the glue soaking through to the front side). Use a mini paint roller or a large sponge to help work the glue over the entire jute surface. You want every single bit of twine covered with glue. Roll the glue around the outside edge, too, which will adhere the fabric all the way around.

9 Once you have a nice, even layer of glue, pull the fabric back over the coil. Starting from the center and moving to the outside edge, press the fabric firmly with your hands, rubbing in small circular motions. You will start to see the coil pattern show through on the fabric. Make sure every surface area has been pressed to fully adhere the fabric to the twine.

10 Repeat on the other side of the rug: Pull back the loose fabric, glue, roll, cover, and press firmly from the center to the outside. Once everything has been securely glued, let the rug sit for at least 24 hours or until fully dry.

11 Turn the rug over so that the painter's tape is facing up. Gently peel off all the tape. Hold the rug down with one hand and peel the tape off slowly with the other. It is best to try to peel in the direction of the coil.

12 Now cut off the excess fabric around the edge by pushing your scissors, halfway open, close to the outside edge of the coiled twine. Hold the scissors with one hand and pull the fabric away from the twine with the other hand. This will spin the rug as the scissors cut the fabric close to the coil. Be careful not to cut through the twine.

13 You can clean this rug by giving it a good shake outside. It is best not to roll this rug up for storage; try to keep it flat.

# painted ceramic tray

I tend to take my jewelry off right after I've climbed in bed. This beautiful gold-leafed tray is the perfect spot to stash these items safely overnight. Having a designated catchall for jewelry and trinkets that end up on your nightstand is a must. You will always know where to look for your rings in the morning as you are rushing out the door. Make sure to purchase or find ceramic dishes that you know are oven-safe. The baking temperature for the ceramic paint isn't very high, but some dishes are not made to withstand much heat and will crack.

SUPPLIES

Oven-safe tray, plate, cup, or bowl in ceramic or
    porcelain
Pébéo Porcelaine 150 paint
Liquid gold leaf in classic gold

TOOLS

2-inch flat paintbrush
Small round paintbrush
Newspapers (optional) or grassy area outside
Safety glasses

**1** Before painting, clean the tray to remove any dirt or oil.

**2** To make a long brushstroke, decide where you would like it to start on the plate and drip out a little paint, right at the brushstroke start point (see Tip).

**3** Take the flat brush and push it down at the edge of the paint, pulling the brush across the plate slowly and trying to keep your brushstroke as straight as possible. As you get to the end of the stroke, start to pick the brush up slightly to soften the edges of the stroke and then pick the brush off the plate completely. Let the paint dry on the tray for 24 hours.

**4** Place the tray in the oven and set the temperature at 300 degrees Fahrenheit. (If you let the tray heat up along with the oven, there is less chance of it cracking.) Bake for 35 minutes. Turn off the oven and let the tray cool in the oven to room temperature.

**5** Add the gold-leaf splatter detail: This is best done outside or in a well-protected and well-ventilated area. Wear your safety glasses while painting. Lay the tray down, faceup. Dip the round brush into the gold paint and start splattering it on the tray by flicking your wrist above the tray. Go in several different directions to create an even splatter across the whole tray. Re-dip the brush as needed. Allow the gold leaf to dry for at least 12 hours before use.

**6** To care for the tray once completed, wash by hand with mild soap and cool water.

**TIP**

**You can create all kinds of patterns using different-size paintbrushes. Go for all-over color or use several colors on 1 tray. Always bake the Pébéo paint on the tray before painting on the gold leaf.**

# acrylic side table

A touch of acrylic can lend light and freshness to any room. I especially love using acrylic for a simple bedside table, which will store books or pillows and blankets underneath while hosting a small lamp and a fresh vase of flowers on top. This project is made of thick-walled, high-quality acrylic, which feels clean and timeless. This table is easily transported from room to room and would look equally as stunning flanking the sofa in the living room or placed in a small entryway. The best part of constructing this project is that no heavy-duty tools are required. Order your acrylic in custom-cut pieces and use an adhesive to put the sides together—simple as that.

## SUPPLIES

¼-inch-thick clear acrylic sheet (see Tip), cut to the following sizes:
- one 16 x 20-inch piece (*top surface*)
- two 16 x 24-inch pieces (*side surfaces*)

Polypropylene funnel (see Tip)

4 ounces TAP acrylic cement (see Tip)

Small BD/2 hypo applicator bottle (see Tip)

## TOOLS

Large flat surfaces joined at a 90-degree angle, for support while building (a wall and flat flooring work great)

Combination square (helpful but not required)

Painter's tape

Rubber gloves

Safety glasses

**TIP**

The acrylic, poly funnel, acrylic cement, and applicator bottle can all be purchased from TAP Plastics (www.tapplastics.com). The folks at TAP Plastics will cut the acrylic for you to the specified sizes at left and can answer any questions you have if you would like to change the measurements of the table to fit your space needs. Also, they sell acrylic in all sorts of great colors, so be adventurous and build a colorful table.

**1** Pieces of acrylic come with protective paper on each side. The smallest piece of acrylic will be the top of your table. Remove 1 side of the paper on this *top surface piece*, but leave 1 side on to keep it from getting scratched as you work. Place the paper side down on the floor, next to a wall that does not have molding at the bottom. Position the 16-inch side against the wall.

**2** Remove the paper from both sides of the larger acrylic *side surfaces*. Stand 1 of the *sides* against the wall, matching the two 16-inch edges together (with the *side surface* on top of the *top surface*). Line up the edges flush against the wall. Use painter's tape to stick the side to the wall, to prevent it from moving as you cement the 2 pieces together. Once you apply the cement, there is no going back, so double-check to make sure that the edges are even and lined up all the way around, and the joint angle is 90 degrees between the top and the side.

**3** Put on your safety gear. Grab the funnel, the acrylic cement, and the applicator bottle. Screw off the top of the applicator bottle and set it aside. Place the funnel into the bottle. Carefully pour the acrylic cement into the bottle until it's about halfway full. Screw the cap on the bottle.

**4** You are going to apply the cement right along the joint, where the side surface edge meets the top surface. To prevent the cement from dripping on the acrylic as you get the bottle into place, tip the bottle upright and squeeze a little air out of the bottle. As you bring the bottle over to the joined acrylic pieces, release the bottle to allow air to flow in and to prevent cement from dripping out. Start on 1 side of the joint, place the applicator needle in the corner, and pull it along the joint, gently squeezing out the cement and allowing it to flow across the bottom of the joint between the 2 pieces. You will see that the edge will become darker as it gets wet. Evenly apply the cement all the way across the joint until you reach the opposite corner.

**5** The bond will form within a matter of minutes. Let it sit for at least 30 minutes to allow any extra cement to evaporate. After the cement is dry, remove the tape and turn the table base around, lining up the opposite 16-inch side of the top surface to the wall.

**6** Place the other side surface on the wall on top of the tabletop surface. Line it up just as you did before. Tape it to the wall and repeat the process of cementing it with the applicator bottle. Let it dry for 30 minutes.

**7** The cement will fully cure in 24 to 48 hours, so don't apply a lot of pressure or move the table too much in the meantime. Peel off the top sticky paper.

**8** The acrylic surface does scratch easily, so be careful in determining its use. You can clean it with a soft damp cloth and a mild nonabrasive soap. Don't use glass cleaner, which can turn the acrylic cloudy over time.

# simple diy: refurbished table lamp

Make sure you have at least one more source of light other than your ceiling fixture. Table lamps or bedside sconces are key to creating the right bedside lighting for the evening hours. Luckily for us, lighting is easy to make! These flush-mount ceiling lights simply needed a drill hole at the base to hold the cord and rewiring to turn them into modern table lamps. They look even better upside down. You can find inexpensive light fixtures at reuse stores, thrift shops, or flea markets. Your local lamp shop or electrician can help you refurbish them.

# boro stitched memory quilt

There is nothing better than a wall brought to life by a cozy quilt, sewn with scraps that carry memories. Gather fabric pieces from your past, like old blankets, a favorite high school T-shirt, or a remnant of your mother's dress. There is no rhyme or reason here when cutting your pieces. Fill up the whole space with different complementary fabrics. This can be a project that you work on for a long time. To make this project even easier, use a premade quilt base and stitch fabric layers on top of it. Kantha quilts work really well for this method.

## SUPPLIES

53 x 60-inch piece of heavyweight fabric, like denim or canvas

15–20 pieces of scrap fabric, with pieces measuring from 18 x 42 inches down to 2½ x 4 inches (I chose vintage pieces of cottons, denims, and homespun)

Clear or invisible thread for machine-stitching

Contrasting-color thread for machine-stitching

7½ yards of trim (see Tip)

Contrasting-color thread for hand-sewing with accompanying sewing needle

3 to 8 eye hooks or soldered jump rings

3 to 8 1-inch nails

## TOOLS

Straight pins

Sewing machine

Scissors

Sewing needle

TIP

I used a ⅞-inch-wide white cotton trim with a decorative edge and dyed it in an indigo vat (see page 204). You can also use single- or double-fold bias tape.

**1** Place the denim, right side up, on the floor. Arrange the scrap fabric, printed side up, on the denim in a pattern of your choosing. Some pieces should overlap and others can be isolated.

**2** Once you are happy with the placement, take a photo or 2, since you will need to remove the pieces for sewing. (This is much faster than pinning and marking.)

**3** Remove all the scrap pieces that are layered on top of other scrap pieces, leaving in place only the scraps that completely touch the denim. Pin those scraps down.

**4** Wind a bobbin with the invisible thread and put it in the sewing machine's bobbin case. Use the contrasting thread for the topstitching only.

**5** Sew the pinned scrap fabrics to the denim, using a long stitch length; this stitch and the invisible thread will help make the stitching appear less machine-made.

**6** When all the pieces are attached, remove the denim from the machine and clip the threads.

**7** Return the denim to the floor and add the next layer of scraps. Repeat the pinning and sewing procedure until all the scraps have been adhered to the denim. You may want to hand-stitch a few of the scraps to the denim to give it more of a handcrafted look.

**8** Place the plain edge of the trim on the back of the quilt and fold it around to the front; pin about 3 inches of the trim to the outer edge. This is to secure the start of the trim to the quilt for proper placement. Once you begin sewing, you can just line up the trim with your hands so you don't have to pin the whole trim. Be sure that you are stitching the front and the back of the trim at the same time. Miter-sew the corners, if you choose.

**9** Cut a piece of contrasting-color thread 18 inches long and thread your sewing needle. Hand-stitch eye hooks or soldered jump rings to the back of the quilt, about ½ inch from the top edge. You can add 3 or more hooks to the back. The more hooks you sew on, the straighter the top edge of the quilt will be once you hang it on the wall.

**10** Place nails in the wall to accommodate the hooks and hang the quilt.

the closet

# copper garment rack

The luster of the copper pipes, mixed with the practicality of the wooden wheels, detailed in leather, create an elegant and timeless piece of furniture. For even more storage, additional items like bags and scarves can be placed on the two long hooks at either end. If you already have ample space to store your clothes, use this as a stunning coatrack in the entryway or as a closet in the guest bedroom. This garment rack is beautiful enough to move freely around your home on wheels, preventing scratched floors.

## SUPPLIES

22 feet of ¾-inch copper pipe, cut as follows (see Tips and page 148):
- two 52-inch pieces (*long sides, A*)
- two 8-inch pieces (*short sides, B*)
- two 44-inch pieces (*top and bottom, C*)
- two 7½-inch pieces (*side hooks, D*)
- two 2¼-inch pieces (*small bottom connectors, E*)
- four 6¼-inch pieces (*wheel casings, F*)
- two 1¼-inch pieces (*bottom wheel connectors, G*)

Tooling cowhide leather, 6- to 7-ounce weight/ thickness, enough to cut four 2¾-inch circles from the hide

Four 5⅛ x ¾-inch-thick, large, pine wood toy wheels (find these at www.caseyswood.com)

Four ⁵⁄₁₆ x 8-inch zinc-plated standard (SAE) hex bolt (bolt thread pinch = 18)

Duct tape

Two ⁵⁄₁₆-inch zinc-plated standard (SAE) regular nuts (nut thread size = 18)

6¾-inch copper pressure tee

4¾ x ¾-inch copper, 90-degree cup x cup pressure elbow

2¾-inch copper tube cap

2-ounce copper lock, no-heat solder

## TOOLS

Large-diameter mini tube cutter

Tape measure

Pencil

Masking tape

Heavy-duty circle cutter

Cutting mat

Electric drill with ⁵⁄₁₆-inch drill bit

Combination wrench

Safety glasses

Sanding sponge (optional)

**TIPS**

• Copper pipe is sold in lots of different lengths. You can get 22 feet by buying 3 pieces of 10-foot pipe, with some extra left over, or by buying a shorter length. Just make sure that you buy a long enough piece to accommodate the larger cuts, like the top, bottom, and sides of the garment rack.

• Type L copper pipe is best, as it is stronger, but you can use type M for lighter garments.

**1** Cut all the copper pipe, specified on page 145, using a tube cutter. Double-check that the like-size pieces are all cut exactly the same length to ensure a balanced build. It is helpful to label the sections with the letters written on a small piece of masking tape and stick them to each cut piece of tubing. This will help avoid confusion when building the garment rack.

**2** Line up the circle cutter on the leather to cut a 2¾-inch circle, which means the blade will be 1⅜ inches away from the center point. Push the circle cutter down on the leather (placed on top of a cutting mat) with enough allowance on the sides of the leather to cut out a full circle. Push down firmly and swing the blade all the way around. While holding the leather in place, cut a circle out fully from the leather. Repeat to cut 3 more leather circles.

**3** Using a drill loaded with a ⁵⁄₁₆-inch drill bit, drill through the center point of each leather circle.

**4** Line up 1 leather circle so that its hole matches up with the center hole of a wooden wheel. Push the threaded side of an 8-inch hex bolt through the leather and the wood hole. The head of the bolt should be resting flush with the leather. Repeat with the remaining pieces of leather and wooden wheels.

**5** Add some thickness to the bolt with duct tape, right beside the wooden wheel. This will help steady the wheel and keep it straight inside the copper pipe. Take a 5-inch piece of duct tape and put the torn end of the tape along the bolt. Coil the duct tape tightly around the bolt. Insert the bolt with the tape into any copper pipe to check the fit. If it goes in easily, you should add a little more tape. If you are struggling to get it into the pipe, take away a little tape. You want a tight fit, but one that goes into the pipe without ripping the tape. Add duct tape to all 4 wheels.

**6** Slide a wheel casing (each bolt with tape) into *copper pipe F*, enclosing the duct tape inside. The pipe should be flush to the wooden wheel. Using the combination wrench, screw 1 nut halfway onto 1 hex bolt. Screw the second nut halfway onto another hex bolt.

**7** Grab a pressure tee and insert 1 of the wheel casings (with the nut attached) into 1 side of the long straight section of the pressure tee. Grab a wheel casing that does not have a nut attached and twist it on the opposite side of the pressure tee. As you are twisting it on, connect the open bolt inside the nut. You can look down through the top of the pressure tee to help guide you. Once the bolt is inserted in the nut, twist only the end of the bolt while holding the other, already-connected bolt steady, to get it to screw into the nut and meet the first inserted bolt. Take the wrench and tighten the 2 sides of the wheel casings together, making sure that both bolts are securely screwed into the nut. Repeat this step to form another identical wheel unit. The wheels will move stiffly at first, but with use the copper pipe will start to cut away a channel, which will help the wheel to spin more smoothly.

**8** Now we are going to build the upper portion of the rack. Twist all the pipes and fittings into place following the diagram on page 148. Twist each copper pipe into the fitting until the pipe stops moving. Lay this form on the floor and make sure everything is lined up straight.

**9** Once the rack is built, you will solder it together. Avoid getting solder on your hands and it is a good idea to wear eye protection. Copper solder works really fast, so it's best to do 1 joint at a time, laying 1 back down flat to dry before moving to another joint. I like to keep the whole rack built and just remove the section that I am going to solder so I know everything is lined up perfectly as the solder dries.

*continues*

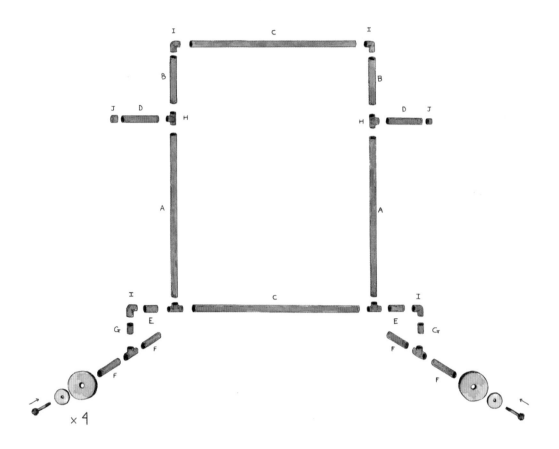

**10** Open the solder and apply a line of solder around each inside rim of the fitting. Twist the pipe a half turn, making sure it is fully inside the fitting and lay it back down flat to dry. Repeat for all joints, waiting at least a minute between each one.

**11** Now, connect the soldered upper portion of the rack to the bottom portion with the wheels. Solder the 2 ends of the *bottom wheel connectors G*, into the top of the pressure tee on each wheel unit. Apply solder around the

rim of each pressure tee. Since we can't give these pipes a half twist, just make extra sure they are pounded all the way to the bottom of the pressure tee and level on both sides. Allow the solder to dry fully before use.

**12** You can give the garment rack a once-over with a sanding sponge to brighten it up. Or leave it roughed up with fingerprints and oxidation. It will oxidize naturally over time.

# simple diy: wall shoe display

Leave your shoes in plain view for easy access by hanging vintage or new molding that's 1 to 2 inches wide. The ball of your shoe should be able to lie flat on the wall. Miter each end of the molding at a 45-degree angle (see page 210). Mount each row of molding to the wall using nails; hammer them in straight from the front, just above the center line. Try to get at least 1 or 2 nails on the same piece of molding into a wall stud for support, and use a level for accurate mounting.

# leaning floor mirror

Floor mirrors are essential when you are planning an outfit. Throw away that cheap college-dorm mirror that hangs on the back of your door and upgrade to this leaning version with stately painted trim. I pulled this glass off an old, outdated mirror, but you can use the glass from any mirror and adjust the cut size of the plywood base and moldings. Be on the lookout for large mirrors at thrift and reuse stores, which usually offer them on the cheap.

## SUPPLIES

Plywood, cut 3 inches larger than your mirror on
    all sides
Mirror
Interior paint in any color (optional)
$\frac{7}{16}$ x $\frac{11}{16}$-inch pine, finger-jointed, shoe-base
    molding (the amount depends on the mirror
    size; see Tip)
1½-inch, 23-gauge headless nails
Copper gold leaf

## TOOLS

Pencil
Tape measure
Water-soaked paper towels
Gorilla Glue in squirt tube
Lots of heavy books
Large flat paintbrush (optional)
Clamping miter box with handsaw
    or an electric miter box
Hammer
Small round paintbrush

**TIP**
Shoe-base molding is sold as a
96-inch-long piece at the hardware
store. If you know your frame and
miter-cut measurements ahead
of time, you can have it cut into
smaller sections at the store
(making sure to accommodate
extra length for mitering corners).

**1** Lay the plywood on a flat surface that can hold a lot of weight, such as a protected floor. Using a pencil, measure and mark a guide to center the mirror on the board.

**2** Lightly dampen the back of the mirror and the middle of the plywood with the water-soaked paper towels. Apply a generous amount of Gorilla Glue within the marked lines on the plywood. Try to stay at least 2 inches from the lines, as Gorilla Glue expands considerably as it dries. Place the mirror, reflection side up, on top of the glue, centered on the plywood. Once the mirror is positioned 3 inches from each side, place an even distribution of heavy books on top to hold the mirror in place as the glue dries. Let it dry for at least 24 hours.

**3** Remove the books. If you would like to paint the edges of the plywood, grab a large flat paintbrush and paint around the mirror and around the plywood edges. You can paint the back of the plywood after the mirror is complete. Let the paint dry completely, at least 8 hours.

**4** Create a frame with the molding to go around the mirror. Cut a 45-degree miter joint at the end of the molding, cutting into the $^{11}\!/_{16}$-inch measurement as it lies flat on the saw. Line up the bottom corner of the miter joint with the top left corner of the mirror, the $^{11}\!/_{16}$-inch side flat on the plywood and the $^7\!/_{16}$-inch side touching your mirror. Your miter joint should be extending up. Hold it in place firmly, and using a pencil, mark on the molding where the start of the opposite bottom corner miter joint needs to be cut. Use your saw to cut the second miter joint, mirroring the direction of the angle of the first cut. Cut another piece of molding exactly the same way for the opposite side of the mirror frame. Set these 2 pieces aside.

**5** Start again cutting a 45-degree miter joint at the end of the uncut molding. Line up the bottom angle of the miter joint even with the upper left corner of the mirror. Hold the molding firmly in place along the edge of the mirror and mark the molding at the bottom left side of the mirror, where the beginning of the miter joint needs to be cut. Cut the joint with the saw.

**6** Grab the 2 pieces of molding you cut in step 4 and line up all 3 pieces of molding on the mirror. Make sure they line up correctly on the mirror, all fitting snuggly around the mirror's edge. You can cut the miter joints on the third piece shorter, if needed. Once the fit is correct, cut another piece of molding the same length as the last cut, mirroring the angles of the miter joints. Now you should have 4 miter-cut pieces of molding that fit snugly together, forming a frame around the mirror.

**7** Lay the molding on the plywood, framing the mirror. Nail the molding to the plywood every 6 to 8 inches, adding at least 1 nail close to each miter joint. Be careful as you nail, going slowly and gently because you don't want to crack the mirror or dent the molding.

**8** Once the molding is firmly nailed in place, tape the edges of the mirror and the painted plywood. Paint on the copper gold leaf using a small round paintbrush. If you'd like, once this has fully dried (after about 3 hours), carefully turn the mirror over and paint the back the same color as you did the plywood front. (This is optional; you won't really be able to see the back of the mirror, but it does add a nice finishing touch.)

# thread-wrapped pendant light

Made of two lampshade frames and a lot of thread, this innovative pendant light couldn't be more stunning or simple. Pick up a couple good movies while making this project because it takes some time to get the wrapping down. When I was finished with this light, I considered dip-dyeing the threaded fixture, but ended up loving the all-white look. If you dip-dye yours, I hope you'll send me a picture, because I want to see!

## SUPPLIES
Two 5 x 12 x 8-inch round lamp frames with
    washer top (www.lampshop.com)
800-yard spool of cotton warp thread (see Tip)
3 x 4-inch piece of cardboard
Lamp cord set (www.sundialwire.com)

## TOOLS
Wire cutters
Scissors
Tapestry needle

TIP
I buy warp thread in a large spool from yarn.com. You will not use it all for this project, but the spool is cheaper to buy than purchasing the thread in smaller amounts.

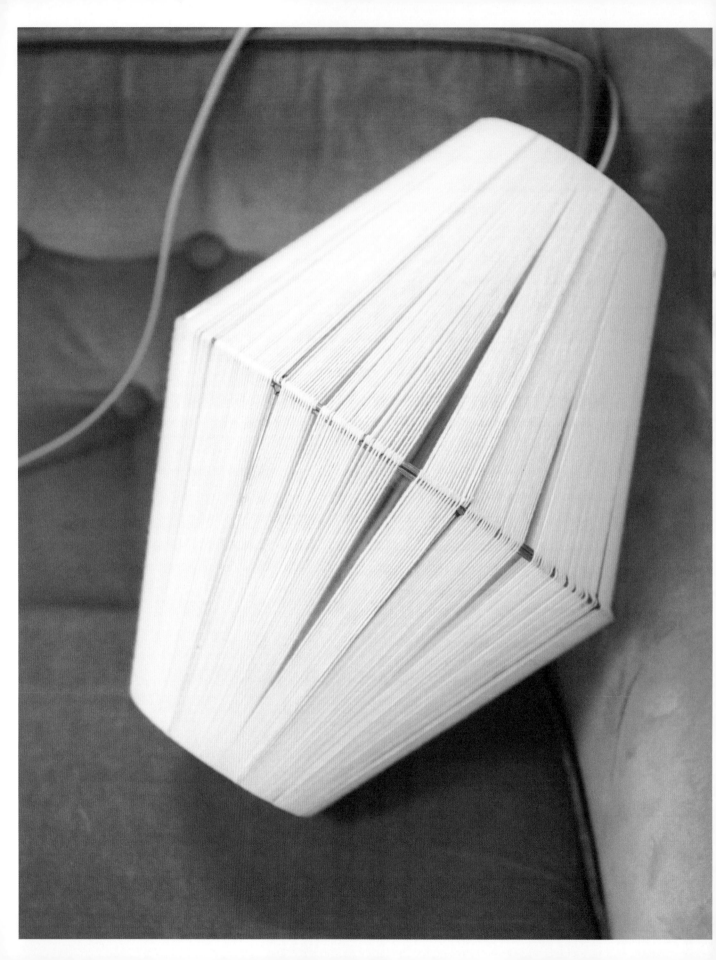

**1** Using the wire cutters, cut the washer top off 1 lamp where it is attached to the top ring, being careful not to bend the frame out of shape as you cut. Leave the second frame as is; do not cut the washer top off.

**2** Take the end of the cotton warp thread and hold it against the center of the small piece of cardboard. Start winding the thread around the cardboard until you have covered the cardboard, leaving ½-inch border of cardboard on either side so the thread doesn't slip off as you are working with it. You want to wrap approximately 10 to 20 yards of thread on the cardboard. Cut the thread from the spool with scissors.

**3** Starting with the lamp frame that still has the washer top intact, tie the end of thread from the cardboard to one of the top washer prongs, close to the outer round rim. Leave a 5-inch tail of thread (you will use this later to tie off the end point).

**4** Starting on the outside of the frame, pull the thread on the cardboard to the bottom of the frame and wrap it around and back up to the starting point on the inside. Keep wrapping it around and around until you have completely filled the top ring with thread. As you wrap it around, make sure the top threads are not crossing over one another but lying flat against the wire, all in a row.

**5** When you run out of thread, wrap another 10- to 20-yard strand around the cardboard spool just as you did in step 2 (you will need to do this several times.) Whenever you start a new spool, always bring the end of the thread that you wrapped on the frame to the inside of the frame and tie the new thread end to the old one with a secure knot so that it's hidden inside. Snip off the tails.

**6** Continue to wrap the entire frame until you have covered the top ring with thread.

**7** When you reach the starting point, tie the end of the thread tightly to the tail you left at the beginning and snip off any tails.

**8** Match up the second wire frame to the larger bottom ring of the thread-wrapped bottom ring. Tie the 2 frames together with a couple of temporary sections of thread to hold them in place as you work. Cut off a 6-yard piece of thread from the spool. Thread it onto the tapestry needle and pull it down about 6 inches.

*continues*

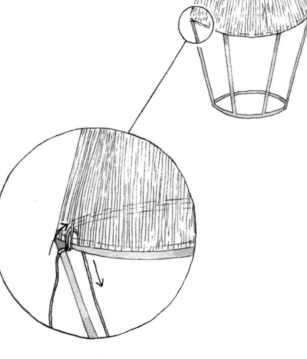

**9** To attach the bottom frame, wrap it almost the same way you wrapped the top, except each time you bring the thread around the frame it will go in between every wrapped thread on the top frame. Poke the needle above the large ring on the top wrapped frame, through any 2 strands of thread. Pull the thread until there is a 2-foot tail. Wrap the end of thread, opposite the needle end, under the bottom frame and tie it to the long end of the thread with the needle, just to hide the knot on the inside and secure the thread as you move around the frame.

**10** Continue wrapping the thread around the bottom frame, over and under, each time going in between the top frame strands. Work in 6-yard sections and knot on new thread as you go, re-threading the needle each time. Try to go slowly when you pull the length of thread at each pass; it can become easily tangled since it is such a long piece.

**11** Work all the way around the frame, until you reach the starting point. Tie the final knot to the inside of the frame to hide the knot. Snip off any tails.

**12** Use the inner washer top to hang the light with a pendant lamp cord. Dangle the light inside halfway down the fixture. Use a lightbulb that's 40 watts or less to avoid overheating the thread.

# liberty print hamper

Good-bye plastic hampers! This beauty will not want to sit behind the door and out of sight. I chose a lively Liberty print to infuse a bit of fun into an otherwise ordinary, everyday object. With wood and leather handles, this stunner is also lightweight and easy to transport, so you won't be ashamed to walk your laundry down to the corner laundromat (I'm looking at you, city dwellers).

### SUPPLIES

4 leather strips, cut to ⁹⁄₁₆ inches wide x 10½ inches long

Two 5 x ½-inch-diameter round wooden dowels

Heavy interfacing, cut as follows:

- Two 22½ x 48-inch pieces
- Two 16-inch-diameter circles

2½ yards of Liberty fabric or cotton print, cut as follows:

- one 25 x 52-inch piece
- one 16-inch-diameter circle

2½ yards of canvas fabric, cut as follows:

- one 25 x 49-inch piece
- one 16-inch-diameter circle

Thread in coordinating color

Nylon upholstery thread in contrasting color for sewing leather

### TOOLS

Small binder clips

E6000 glue

Iron

Tape measure

Straight pins

Sewing machine

Tailor's chalk

Leather needle for sewing machine

**1** Fold 1 leather strip over each wooden dowel lengthwise so that the ends of the leather meet. Using a small binder clip, join the 2 sides together, leaving a bit of ease to slide out the dowel. Repeat this on the opposite side of the dowel. Remove the dowels, keeping the clips in place.

**2** Put a small amount of glue on 1 end of a dowel and very gently ease the dowel back between the leather. Repeat with the opposite side. Be careful not to get any glue on the exposed leather. Glue the leather to the second dowel the same way. Set aside and let the glue dry for at least 12 hours.

**3** Iron an interfacing circle to the wrong side of the Liberty circle. Iron an interfacing circle to the wrong side of the canvas circle.

**4** Iron an interfacing panel to the wrong side of the Liberty panel. (Several inches of the Liberty fabric will not be interfaced.) Iron an interfacing panel to the wrong side of the canvas panel.

**5** Double over the long piece of canvas with the interfacing side out. Pin the 49-inch side and sew a ⅜-inch seam from the top to the bottom. Secure with several anchor stitches on each side.

**6** Place the canvas bottom in the newly created canvas tube with the interfacing facing out. Pin the circle to the tube in 8 places, with the pins spaced evenly around.

**7** Using a short basting stitch, begin machine-stitching the tube seam with a ³⁄₁₆-inch seam allowance. Gently guide the fabric underneath the presser foot, easing in the fabric as needed. Once you've completed the circle, remove the fabric from the sewing machine and make sure everything is sewn properly. Return to the machine, reset the stitch length to medium, and sew again around the bottom circle, using a ½-inch seam allowance.

**8** Double over the long piece of Liberty fabric with the interfacing side out. Pin the 52-inch side and sew a ⁵⁄₁₆-inch seam from the top to the bottom, beginning and ending with several anchor stitches.

**9** Position the Liberty bottom into the newly created tube with the interfacing facing out. Pin the circle to the tube in 8 places, with the pins spaced evenly around.

**10** Using a short basting stitch, begin machine-stitching the tube seam with a ³⁄₁₆-inch seam allowance. Gently guide the fabric underneath the presser foot, easing in the fabric as needed. Once you've completed the circle, remove the fabric from the sewing machine and make sure everything is sewn properly. Return to the machine, reset the stitch length to medium, and sew again around the bottom circle, using a ½-inch seam allowance.

**11** Fold over ½ inch of the top of the Liberty fabric and iron. Turn the Liberty tube right side out. Place the canvas tube inside the Liberty tube and smooth the fabric.

**12** Now fold over the extra Liberty fabric to the inside of the tube so that it forms a cuff over the canvas. Sew a ¼-inch seam on the folded edge of the Liberty fabric.

**13** Flatten the upper tube in half, making sure that the seam is a few inches from the side fold. Find the center and mark it with tailor's chalk. From the center point, measure to the right and left 2⅝ inches, and mark the 2 places with pins. Remove the center pin.

**14** When the glue on the leather strip handles has dried fully, remove the clips. Place 1 side of the leather on the handles where the right pin is located. There should be 2½ inches of leather tucked over the top of the tube. Secure with a binder clip.

*continues*

**15** Put the leather needle on your sewing machine. Set the stitch length to 6 stitches per inch. The first stitch will be taken from the top of the tube at the center of the leather; leave a long tail on the top and bottom threads. Stitch along the center of the leather 2 inches, leaving a long tail on the top and bottom threads. Repeat these steps for the other side of the handle.

**16** Remove the clips from the right and left sides. Pull the tails to the reverse side and knot them.

**17** Position the laundry bag in the sewing machine to make a diagonal stitch on the leather strip. This seam will be located ½ inch up from the bottom of the leather—just meeting the center stitch.

**18** The first stitch sewn will be ¼ inch above the right-hand leather piece, traveling across the leather and ending up on the fabric. Secure with several anchor stitches on the fabric but not on the leather. Repeat this step for the left-hand side of the handle.

**19** Pull any tails to the reverse side and knot. Repeat the process for the handle on the reverse side.

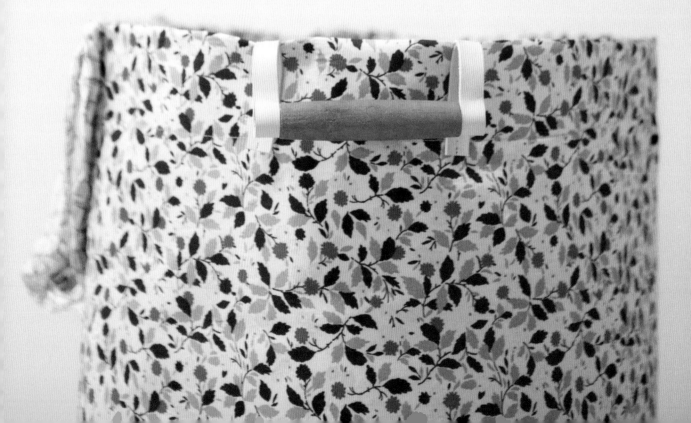

# antiqued mirror table

The sleek style of this table, combined with the textural depth created with these DIY antiqued mirrors, is the perfect blend of old and new. The base of the table is a simple wooden cube, which provides form and stability. If you'd like to complete this project with antiqued mirrors, flip to page 212 for the full tutorial. Otherwise, you can use the mirrors straight out of the box for a more contemporary look.

## SUPPLIES

½-inch-thick piece of plywood (a little more than
    4 x 4 total), cut into the following sizes:
- One 12-inch square (*top, A*)
- Two 11 x 11½-inch pieces (*short sides, B*)
- Two 11½ x 12-inch pieces (*long sides, C*)

4 cut wood legs, each measuring
    1½ x 1½ x 3 inches

Can of flat black spray paint

Five 12 x 12-inch, beveled-edge mirrors (if desired,
    antique them first, using the techniques found
    on page 212)

Tube of Beacon 527 Glue, or strong epoxy glue

## TOOLS

Pencil

Wood glue

Two 24-inch bar clamps

Tape measure

Nail gun with 1¼-inch nails (alternatively, you
    can use a hammer and nails, but this is much
    harder to manage)

Wood stain (optional)

Sheet of 120-grit sandpaper

Drop cloth, old newspapers, or scrap plastic

Heavy books

**1** To build the open bottom cube, first label with a pencil which pieces are the sides and which is the top.

**2** Put 1 of the *C boards* on a flat surface with a 12-inch side facing you. Add a line of wood glue to one 11½-inch edge of 1 *B board*. Place the *B board*, glue side down, at the left edge of the *C board*. Line up the corners and make sure the 2 outside edges meet up perfectly. Repeat on the other side with the second *B board*. The box should look like a "U" at this point. Grab a friend if you need help holding the sides in place as you work.

**3** Add glue to the top edges (the 11½-inch lengths) of the *B boards* and place the second *C board* on top, lining up all the edges. All outside measurements should now be 12 inches.

**4** Pull the box forward, with a quarter of it sticking off the table. Use bar clamps to clamp the *C boards* tightly, which will apply pressure to the glued joints as they dry. The clamps should be placed about 1½ inches from each edge. (If you put the clamps in the middle, the pressure might warp the box as it dries.) Check again to make sure that everything is lined up and all outside measurements are 12 inches.

**5** While the glue is drying, reinforce the joints by shooting a nail every 2 inches on the edge of both *C boards*, where they meet the *B boards*. Wait for the glue to dry overnight.

**6** Remove the clamps and turn the box over so that the opening is pointed toward the ceiling. Place the top board, *A*, on top of the box. Line up all the edges.

**7** Shoot a nail about every 2 inches around all 4 top edges.

**8** Nail in the legs: Measure and mark the middle point (1½ inches) on each leg with a pencil. This is where the leg will line up on the outside edge of the box. Push 1 leg into 1 corner until you reach the 1½-inch mark. Shoot 2 nails into each side of the box to secure the legs in place. Repeat on all 4 corners. If you desire, you can stain or paint the legs any color you like.

**9** Sand the box to remove any splinters.

**10** Outside or on top of a drop cloth, spray-paint all edges of the box with black spray paint. (This will help disguise the meeting points between the mirrors if your box is a little uneven.)

**11** Glue the mirrors on, one at a time, starting with the very top mirror: Apply a generous amount of 527 glue over the entire top of the plywood surface, avoiding the edges so the glue won't seep out. Place the first mirror, right side up, on top of the glue and wiggle it just a little to evenly coat both surfaces. Line up all 4 edges and corners to match the box. Place some heavy books on top to compress it while drying. Let this dry for 3 hours before moving to the other sides.

**12** As you glue on each new mirror surface, flip the cube so that the mirror you are gluing is facing up. Allow each surface to dry at least 3 hours before moving to the next side. Allow the whole box to dry for at least 24 hours before use.

the bathroom

# natural wood stump

For this project, search your local listings for neighbors who are offering wood cut from a tree they are removing from their yard. Local tree-cutting services often have a plethora of fresh-cut stumps for free or really cheap. You can use these stumps individually in the bathroom or in pairs flanking your sofa. Better yet, cluster a few together to create a unique coffee table. If you do find extra wood, you might as well have more than one stump cut. If you would like to try a painted version, flip to page 186 for inspiration.

SUPPLIES

Tree stump that measures approximately
  20 x 14 inches (see Tip)
Water-based wood stain in color of your choice

TOOLS

1-inch chisel
Hammer
Vibrating palm sander with sanding discs
Damp rag
Flat paintbrush
Shop towel

TIP
You can cut your own tree stump with a chain saw (or have someone with experience do it for you). Seek out already fallen trees; don't cut any live trees.

**1** If the stump you're using has been recently cut, let it dry out completely. Best to leave it alone in a warm and dry place. This could take anywhere from 2 months to a year, depending on the size of your stump and the type of wood. The bark will peel away easily with your hands or a chisel once the stump is fully dry.

**2** When you are ready to remove the bark, use a chisel and, if necessary, a hammer. Take off little sections of bark one at a time, being careful not to go too deeply or you will make scratches and dents in the wood surface.

**3** Go over the entire surface with a palm sander until the surface is smooth. You may need more than 1 sanding disc to complete the job. Smooth out the top surface as much as possible, making circular motions with the sander to remove chain-saw marks, if any. (I like a few marks for character.) Sand around the top edge to bevel or angle it for a more polished look. Sand all around the sides and, if you wish, bevel the bottom edge. When you're done, use a damp rag to wipe off all the dust.

**4** Paint on a layer of stain evenly over the entire wood surface (no need to stain the bottom). Wipe off the excess stain with a shop cloth. Let the stain dry for 2 hours and add more coats, if needed. Once you like the color, let the stain dry for 24 hours before using.

# oak tub tray

Stained oak-wood planks come together to create a naturally beautiful storage solution for your tub. Prop up a good book, light a couple votive candles, and place a glass of wine right on the tray for a truly wonderful and relaxing bath. Make sure to seal the wood surface for long-lasting wear.

## SUPPLIES

Three X x 3½ x ½-inch oak boards (see Tip)

Two 9 x ¾ x 2-inch wood slats (oak will match the top surface, but if you are going to stain the tray, the type of wood won't matter, since these will be on the underside)

Wood stain (optional), any color

Water-resistant wood sealant (matte or glossy finish)

## TOOLS

Tape measure

Pencil

Sheet of 150-grit sandpaper

Damp rag

Wood glue

Heavy books

Rag for stain application

Flat paintbrush

TIP

This measurement of X is based on your tub's width. Measure the width of your tub, from outer edge to outer edge, and adjust this measurement accordingly.

**1** Measure the inside width of your tub (see Tip on page 167). Write down this measurement, which you will use in step 4.

**2** Sand all the edges of the boards until smooth and free of splinters. Wipe away sawdust with a damp rag.

**3** Line up the 3 boards together, horizontally, with all long sides together and on a flat surface. Find the center of the boards using a tape measure and make a light pencil mark there.

**4** Divide your inner tub measurement in half. Starting at the marked center of the boards, measure out the length you just got and mark with a pencil. This is where the outer edge of one of the bottom slats will lie. The slats will keep the tray from sliding off your tub's edge and falling into the water.

**5** Apply a generous amount of wood glue to 1 side of a slat. Center it, glue side down (perpendicular to the length), across the 3 boards and to the inside of the marked line you just created. Repeat on the other side of the board with the second slat.

**6** After 30 minutes, very carefully turn the board over and apply some weight to the top (heavy books work well), to help the boards clamp down as they dry. Allow the glue to dry overnight.

**7** If desired, you can apply an overall wood stain to the tray with a rag. Let it dry for 24 hours.

**8** Seal the board to protect it from moisture, using a water-resistant sealant. Apply a light, even coat over the whole board with a flat paintbrush. Allow it to dry for 24 hours before use.

# knotted rope ladder

This stunningly simple wood-and-cotton rope ladder is a wonderful way to store towels, blankets, magazines, and even jewelry. Its tall, slender design adds versatility to tight spaces. Not only is it a smart storage solution, but it also looks like an art object itself when unadorned. Lean this near your sink for easy towel access, transport it to the living room to hang quilts, or place it next to your bed to keep magazines and books within easy reach.

## SUPPLIES

Two 1¼ x 72-inch round wood dowels

2 scrap pieces of wood, same thickness, to hold your dowels while drilling

Two ¾ x 15-inch round wood dowels

12 feet of ½ inch thick triple-twisted cotton rope in natural white

## TOOLS

Tape measure

Pencil

Electric drill with ¾-inch spade drill bit and ⅝-inch drill bit

Sheet of 120-grit sandpaper

Wood glue

Scissors

Masking tape

**1** On each 72-inch wood dowel, draw a straight line from top to bottom. This line will help guide your hole placement. All drilled holes should be made along this line.

**2** Measure 3 inches down from each end of the 2 large dowels and make a mark with a pencil (along the long line you made on the dowel). The holes for the smaller wood dowels will be drilled at these marks.

**3** Load your drill with the ¾-inch drill bit. The holes for the smaller dowels need to go only halfway through the large dowel. Keep an eye on how far the spade bit goes into the wood so that it doesn't pop out on the other side. Drill the 2 holes on each dowel, making sure you keep all the holes along the straight line on the same side.

**4** Next, mark where the holes for the rope will need to be drilled on each long dowel. Measure 11 inches down from the center of one ¾-inch hole and mark the placement on the long dowel. Continue all the way down, spacing the holes 11 inches apart so that you end up with 5 hole placements for the rope on each dowel. Hold both dowels up next to each other to check that the marks for hole placements are the same height on each side.

**5** Load your drill with the ⅝-inch drill bit. Since these holes are going to be drilled all the way through the dowel, place a piece of scrap wood under each dowel as you drill, right where the hole will poke through. This will prevent the wood dowel from splintering on the drill exit. Place the other piece of scrap wood under the other side to hold the dowel level so the drill goes straight through and not at an angle.

**6** Drill all 10 holes for your rope. Sand down the hole openings to remove any splinters and to soften the edges.

**7** Apply some wood glue inside the top and bottom ¾-inch holes on each large dowel. Twist the ¾-inch dowels into place, connecting the long dowels together. Leave this someplace flat to dry overnight. Sand off any leftover glue once dry.

**8** Cut 5 sections of rope, about 27 inches each. Roll masking tape over the rope, right where you cut it, to keep it from fraying. Cut it right at the center of the tape. This will also help you easily slide the ends of the rope into each hole.

**9** Push 1 piece of rope through each matching set of holes and tie a knot in the rope on the outer side of each dowel. You can make the rope as taut or loose as you would like. Keep in mind that, since it is cotton, the rope will stretch a bit when something is placed on it.

**10** Trim the ends of the rope to your liking and fray the ends by pulling the triple twist apart with your fingers.

# terry-cloth towels

I like my towels to be large, soft, and absorbent. This project offers all three and has the added benefit of pattern and color. These towels feel cozy, calling out to you like snugly blankets, ready to warm you as soon as you emerge from the shower. Make sure to check the quality of the terry cloth before purchasing it. You want to find cloth that doesn't snag and pull at the slightest tug. Also, be sure to prewash all your fabrics. If you don't, once sewn together they will shrink at different speeds, causing the towels to look warped.

### SUPPLIES

*For the Washcloth*
14 x 14-inch printed, lightweight cotton, prewashed
12 x 12-inch terry-cloth fabric, prewashed
Thread in coordinating color

*For the Bath Towel*
32 x 62-inch printed, lightweight cotton,
    prewashed
10 x 58-inch terry-cloth fabric, prewashed
Thread in coordinating color

### TOOLS

Iron
Sewing machine
Scissors

**1** Make the washcloth: Lay the cotton, right side down, on a work surface. Iron in a 1-inch crease on all 4 sides of the cotton fabric. Position the terry cloth inside the ironed creases.

**2** Sew a double-folded seam, enclosing the raw edge of the terry cloth inside the cotton on 1 vertical side with a ¼-inch seam. Repeat on the opposite side.

**3** Repeat steps 1 and 2 on the other sides, making sure to enclose the edge seams you sewed in step 2. Snip the ends of the thread.

**4** Sew an anchor stitch in the middle of the washcloth, joining the terry cloth and the printed cotton.

**5** Make the bath towel: Repeat steps 1 through 4, with the fabrics specified for the bath towel. Sew 4 more anchor stitches in the towel at the quadrants to secure the 2 fabrics together.

# leather wastebasket

Making a wastebasket attractive was a task I definitely wanted to take on when approaching the bathroom. Does anyone else hate touching the side of the wastebasket when picking it up for trash removal? Here's a simple solution—a loop! The base of this basket is made out of an everyday tin, the kind you buy holiday popcorn in. This wastebasket is so pretty it can easily hang out under your office desk or beside your bedside table. Paint the interior of the tin any color you want. Go for a bright color or tone it down with all-over black or white.

## SUPPLIES

Spray paint in any color

Large round tin can, lid removed

Tooling cowhide leather, 6- or 7-ounce weight/
   thickness, enough leather to cover the outside
   of the can (see Tip)

Four 1- to 2-inch strips of scrap fabric at least
   36 inches long

## TOOLS

Soft tape measure

Cutting mat

Ruler

Pencil

60 mm rotary cutter

Tube of E6000 glue

Paper towels

2 clothespins

**TIP**

To make sure you're getting enough leather for this project, purchase a single shoulder of 6 to 7 square feet, which would leave you with some extra leather for other projects throughout this book. Leather in this quantity may be purchased from tandyleather.com.

**1** Spray-paint the inside of the can any color you would like. Give it at least 2 to 3 light coats. Allow the paint to dry fully, about 1 hour, before moving to the next step.

**2** Using a soft tape measure, measure the outside circumference of the can. Add ¼ inch to this measurement; this will be your leather's length. Now measure the length of the can from the top lip to the bottom. Add ¼ inch to this measurement; this will be the leather's width.

**3** Lay the leather hide, right side down, on the cutting mat. Measure and mark with a pencil the length and width from step 2. Using a ruler along each straight edge, cut out all 4 sides with the rotary cutter. Wrap the rectangle around the can and see if the length measurement meets closely. If the leather overlaps at the back, you will need to cut a tiny bit off so that it lies flat against the can. If there is a small separation, this is okay, as we will cover it up with the long loop.

**4** Lay flat the 4 strips of scrap fabric horizontally on your cutting mat, separating them a couple inches apart. Put the rectangular leather right side down, on top of the fabric strips. Grab the E6000 glue and apply a generous amount of glue over the entire outside of the tin can. (Do not apply glue to the bottom base of the can.) Center the can over the leather and line it up, bottom edges together. The top edge should have the extra ¼ inch sticking over the can.

**5** Wrap the leather around the can, making sure the bottom edge stays even. When it is in place, secure it by wrapping and tying the 2 ends of each fabric strip together. The strips will hold the leather in place as it dries. If any glue seeps out, wipe it away with a paper towel, trying not to get it on the front of the leather. Allow the glue to fully cure for 24 to 48 hours.

**6** In the meantime, cut the leather strip that will be used as the loop. Add 7 inches to the width measurement. This will be the total length of the strip. I cut my width at 1¼ inches, but you can make this wider or narrower. Just make sure that the strip will hide any open area on the can if you have space between the ends of the leather covering. Cut this strip out, using a cutting mat, ruler, and rotary cutter.

**7** Once the leather cover on the can is fully dry, remove the fabric strips and set them aside. Line up the leather strip from the bottom of the can to the top, right over where the 2 ends of the leather can covering meet.

**8** Apply a little glue right to the center of the leather cover, where the 2 ends meet. Add enough glue to adhere to the strip. Place the strip, even with the bottom, and straight up to the top. Once in position, tie the fabric strips around the can and knot them in place to hold the leather strip in position as it dries.

**9** Loop the top part of the strip around the top edge of the leather covering. Apply a little glue just inside where the 2 sections meet. Use 2 clothespins, 1 on each side, to hold the loop in place as it dries. Let the can fully cure for 24 to 48 hours before use. When it is dry, remove the fabric strips and clothespins.

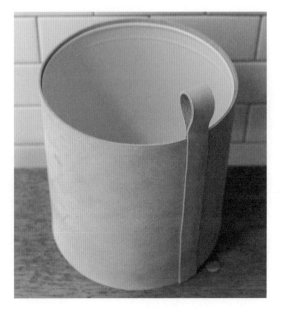

# the outdoor oasis

# simple sewn hammock

The rhythmic swinging of a hammock can be a major stress reliever. In fact, make this project first and then lounge in it while contemplating the rest of your DIY ventures! If you don't have two trees to mount your hammock on, there are hammock stands readily available. Hammocks and swings are also popping up in family rooms all over the country (bring it in, if you dare!). Just make sure to consult with a professional about the strength of your walls and/or ceiling, and whether reinforcement is needed. Don't forget to pile on the pillows and blankets for a truly nap-worthy spot.

## SUPPLIES

3 yards of 60-inch heavyweight linen or cotton
 duck fabric, cut to 60 x 92 inches

Two 14 x 2 x 2-inch wood blocks

Fiber-reactive or acid dye in cool blue

Spool of extra strong nylon upholstery thread in
 coordinating color

Heavy-duty sewing machine needle, size 110/18

Two 48 x 1¼-inch round wooden dowels

Scrap pieces of wood

50 feet of ⅜-inch nylon rope, with a 525-pound
 load limit or more (see Tip)

Two ⅜ x 3½-inch spring links

## TOOLS

Sewing machine

Two 12-inch, clutch-style bar clamps

Iron

Straight pins

Tape measure

Fabric marker

Scissors

Sewing needle

Electric drill with ⅜-inch drill bit

Sheet of 150-grit sandpaper

Masking tape

**TIP**

The rope used in this hammock
has a 525-pound load limit, but the
hammock is best used by just one
person at a time. If you have more
than one person in the hammock
at once, you risk breaking the
hammock. When in doubt, have
your hammock professionally
installed to ensure safety.

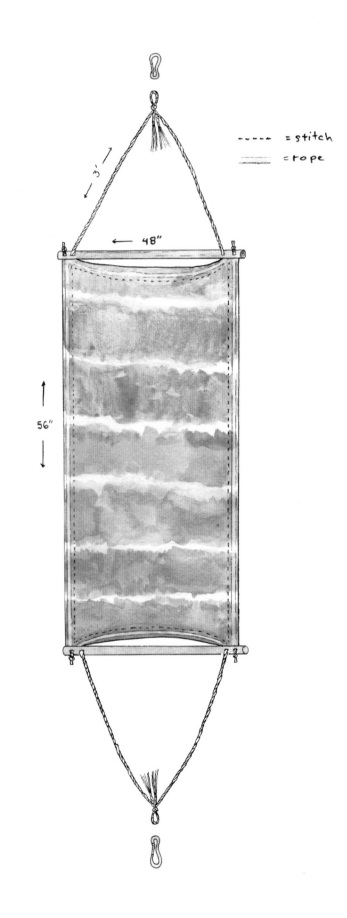

----- = stitch

----- = rope

3'

← 48"

↑
56"
↓

**1** First dye the fabric: Stitch a zigzag edge around all 4 sides to prevent fraying. Lay the fabric down flat on a clean surface. Accordion-fold (see page 206) the fabric, in 6-inch sections, all the way across the length of the fabric. Then fold the whole accordion-folded fabric into thirds so that 1 side folds toward the center and 1 side folds away from the center. The side should look like a squashed Z.

**2** Place 1 wood block on the top and 1 wood block on the bottom of the fabric bundle, lengthwise. Use the clamps at the edge of the blocks to tighten them down on the fabric, creating a resist from the dye. Wet the fabric completely with water. Place the bundle in a dye vat (see page 197), and let it sit until the desired color is reached. Remove the fabric, wash, and dry.

**3** Fold the raw edge of the fabric over 1 inch on a long side and iron to make a crease. Fold the raw edge of the fabric into the crease and iron. Pin for sewing.

**4** With the bulk of the fabric facing away from the sewing machine, stitch 1⁄16-inch from the second folded edge, beginning and ending with a few anchor stitches. Repeat steps 3 and 4 for the opposite long side.

**5** Repeat steps 3 and 4 for the short sides of the fabric, taking care that the raw edges are tucked in at the corners.

**6** With the right side down, measure 4 inches from each corner and add a mark to indicate the beginning of each seam. The 4 inches at the corners will be free from any more stitching.

**7** With the right side down, fold the fabric over 1¼ inches and pin. Begin sewing a seam at the 4-inch mark, using several anchor stitches ⅜ inch from the interior fold. Repeat for the opposite long side of the fabric.

**8** Repeat for the 2 short sides of the fabric. Trim the threads. Now you have all 4 casings done for the rope.

**9** Thread the sewing needle with 30 inches of coordinating thread. Match the 2 thread ends and tie a knot. Hand-sew a large X at the beginning and end of each seam. Make sure you knot the thread well when you have completed the X. Trim any tails.

**10** Measure and mark 1½ inches and then 3 inches from the end of the dowels. Make sure the marks are along the same plane so that the holes are all drilled in the same direction.

**11** Load the drill with a ⅜-inch drill bit. Lay a scrap piece of wood under the dowel where the holes are marked. Drill 4 holes all the way through each dowel; these holes will hold the ropes. As you drill through the dowel, this scrap piece will prevent the wood from splintering. You can place another piece of scrap wood on the opposite side of the dowel to keep it level as you drill. Sand down any splinters.

**12** Cut 4 sections of rope: 2 pieces that measure 12½ feet (to make the inner top loops) and 2 pieces that measure 9½ feet (to make the outer long sides). To cut the rope, wrap a piece of tape around the rope at the measured length and then cut right in the middle of the tape. This will prevent the rope from unraveling while you work.

**13** The rope specified in the supplies list is really silky and can just slide down the fabric seam with a little push and pull. Hold the hammock up straight as you push the rope in; it will eventually pop out the other side. If you are using a different rope and it won't slide in easily, you can tape a long, straight, round dowel to the end of the rope to help guide the rope through the channel.

**14** Thread the 9½ foot rope down the seam of 1 long side of the hammock until it is centered; repeat on the other side with the second 9½ foot rope. Insert the 12½-foot ropes, one through the channel of each short end of the hammock. Center the ropes in the channel.

*continues*

**15** Lay the hammock flat on the ground. Line up the holes of a dowel by the ropes. Thread the 2 ends of the 9½-foot ropes through each outer hole. Tie a simple knot at each end, above the dowel. Leave a 2- to 3-inch tail at the end of each knot.

**16** The rope from the top short side of the hammock will go through the inner holes of a dowel. Pull each rope end into its hole and match up the ends, about 2 feet above the center point of the dowel; the rope length on each side will be about 3 feet. Hold this spot in place with a piece of tape, wrapped around the 2 pieces of rope.

**17** Make an overhand loop knot (see illustration on page 182) above the tape. As you tighten the knot, try to get it as close to the tape as possible. Tighten the rope. The rope will tighten on its own during the first use, but it should be secure before hanging so that the rope doesn't slide.

**18** Repeat to add the dowel and tie the same knots on the opposite side of the hammock. The trick to this side is that you want to pull the 9½-foot rope way down so that there is a little bunching on the long side seams.

**19** Trim off the tape at each end of rope and fray the ends. Make sure you leave at least 2 inches of rope after each knot. Leave at least 4 inches of rope for the top overhand-loop knots.

**20** Attach a spring link inside the overhand loop knot on each side.

# simple diy: painted wood stump

Take the Natural Wood Stump (page 165) one step further with an
all-over coat of color. After finishing the stump, apply a latex-
or oil-based wood primer with a paintbrush before painting
the stump with exterior paint in any color you wish.

# ice-dyed blanket

Ice-dying is one of my all-time favorite methods of achieving stunning color patterns on otherwise plain materials. I picked up this lightweight cotton gauze fabric, knowing that it would be the perfect material to keep me comfortable and cozy while hanging outdoors on a cool night.

## SUPPLIES

2 yards of cotton gauze fabric (try to find fabric with a width of 58 to 60 inches)

Soda ash

Plastic sheeting or drop cloth

5 pound bag of ice

2 tablespoons rose red fiber-reactive dye

2 tablespoons jade green fiber-reactive dye

1 tablespoon rust brown fiber-reactive dye

1 tablespoon clear sky blue fiber-reactive dye

½ tablespoon orange sherbet fiber-reactive dye

Tassel fringe trim in cream, 122 inches, cut in half

Thread in coordinating color

## TOOLS

Scissors

Large plastic storage box

Wire cooling rack (1 large enough to span the whole top of the box, or you can have 2 and overlap them on top of the box)

Rubber gloves, safety glasses, and face mask (to wear when using soda ash and powder dye)

Small plastic pot or container (to soak the fabric in with soda ash)

Measuring spoons

Sewing machine

**1** Ice-dye your fabric following the dyeing instructions on page 201. I've listed the colors on page 187 that I used to create this palette. Hand-wash your fabric and line-dry.

**2** Cut the fabric to 58 x 60 inches.

**3** Sew the blanket by following the Trimmed Waffle-Weave Blanket tutorial on page 122.

# restored-frame tray

When you need to sneak some snacks outside or must have a flat surface to read your magazines, you can easily turn a picture frame into a tray with surprisingly little effort. I found this carved wood frame at a flea market for pennies. It came with glass, which is what you want. If you find a frame without glass, you can purchase replacement glass from your local framing shop or cut your own sheet to size using a handheld glass cutter. I love utilizing these trays indoors or outdoors. An alternative option to topping your tray with galvanized tin is to spray-paint the underside of your glass with any color you like (check out the one sitting on the Dyed Fabric Ottoman on page 36).

SUPPLIES

Carved wood frame (see Tip)

Can of white spray paint and primer in one

Galvanized tin sheet or aluminum sheet, cut to the
    same size as your frame glass

TOOLS

Drop cloth

Metal clippers

TIP

Vintage frames often include wire hanging hardware. Remove this first before beginning this project.

**1** Take the glass out of the frame and set it aside. On top of a drop cloth, spray-paint the entire frame—front, back, and sides. Let it dry for at least an hour.

**2** Cut the galvanized tin to the size of the glass with the metal clippers. Place it on top of the glass, and insert it, tin side up, back into the frame. Secure with the frame's hooks.

# color-wash sheepskin

I love sheepskins around the home. They add a ton of texture and are simply the coziest. They can sit on the arm of your sofa, hang out on the floor as a fluffy rug, or lie on the back of your dining chairs. I started playing around with dyeing them a couple years ago and I've tried a myriad of methods. I like the look and consistency I get by using fiber-reactive dyes. For best results, use a white sheepskin, which will make the dyes truer in color. Feel free to change up the color, as long as you stick with the same type of dye.

## SUPPLIES

4 tablespoons of Dharma Trading clear sky fiber-
    reactive dye
8 tablespoons noniodized salt
Sheepskin, about 3 square feet in size (Ikea sells
    an inexpensive version that you can test before
    dyeing a more expensive sheepskin)

## TOOLS

Two 5-gallon buckets, or larger for a larger
    sheepskin (a kiddie pool works well)
Rubber gloves, safety glasses, and face mask
Glass measuring cup
Large wooden spoon (not used for food
    preparation)
Pet brush

**TIPS**

• Do not use boiling water or dry
the sheepskin on high heat. You
will end up with a felted mass of
wool, impossible to repair.

• Access to an outdoor hose is
helpful for this project.

1 Make your dye mixture in a 5-gallon plastic bucket. Put on your safety gear. In the glass measuring cup, add the dye powder and 1 cup of lukewarm water (see Tips, opposite). Stir the mixture until the powder is fully dissolved. Pour the mixture into the plastic bucket.

2 Mix together the salt and 1 cup of lukewarm water in the glass measuring cup (see Tips, opposite). Stir until dissolved. Pour into the plastic bucket. Add 3 gallons of water to the bucket and stir until thoroughly combined.

3 Push the sheepskin, fur side down, into the bucket. Poke the sheepskin with a wooden spoon until the whole skin is covered with the dye bath. If necessary, you can add a little more water.

4 Leave the sheepskin in the dye bath until you are satisfied with the color. The color will be much lighter when dry, so it is best to leave it in a little longer than you think. I like to leave mine in for at least 30 minutes and up to 2 hours. Stir and poke occasionally so that the dye bath moves around and covers the wool fibers evenly.

5 Pull the sheepskin from the vat; it will be very heavy. Let it drain above the vat for a minute to remove excess water weight. Put the sheepskin in the second plastic bucket. If you are working outdoors and have a hose, rinse the skin (see Tips, opposite). If not, take the sheepskin inside and rinse it out in the bathtub or a work sink under cool water, until the water runs clear. Squeeze out all the excess water you can.

6 Hang the sheepskin up to dry or, if you have a dryer with an air-fluff setting, you can use this to speed up the drying process. The air should not be hot (see Tips, opposite)! You will need to dry it for about 2 to 3 hours on air-fluff. Remove the sheepskin and tug on the hide portion to reshape and soften it. Make sure the sheepskin is fully dry before use or putting it on any furniture.

7 Leave the texture of the wool as is or use a pet brush to fluff it up. If necessary, you can wash the sheepskin in a very mild soap and dry as above.

techniques

# fabric dyeing

Dyeing your own fabrics is extremely rewarding! I love to purchase cloth in white and natural tones, then come up with my own colors and patterns, using the techniques outlined below. Dyeing can become an addictive process. You will start to look around your home when you realize all the possibilities this new hobby holds.

The process of adding color to fabric and fibers is dyeing. Typically, dyeing is done with a special solution containing dyes as well as additional chemicals. Controlling the temperature and time are two key factors in dyeing, as well as using the correct dye and technique for the material you are dyeing. There are mainly two classes of dye—natural dyes (mostly from plants) and human-made dyes. Not all fibers will take on dye the same way. Before approaching a project, make sure that you know what your fabric content is and the correct type of dye that should be chosen for the job. I've presented a general list on page 198, but it is always a good idea to do a test swatch before dyeing the bulk of your fabric or fiber.

## NOTES ON SAFETY

Read all instructions and cautions on the product packaging carefully before use. Whenever you are working with chemicals, always take the necessary precautions. Wear rubber gloves and safety glasses to minimize contact with your hands, eyes, ears, nose, and throat. Always work outside or in a well-ventilated area and wear an organic vapor respirator while mixing the dye. Utensils used for dyeing should never be used for food preparation. Keep out of the reach of children. Empty any unused natural dyes down the sink and flush with cold water. Properly dispose of chemicals in accordance with your local and state regulations.

## Projects in this book feature the following dyes:

### Chemical

**Acid dyes:** These are basic dyes found in any craft or big-box store, with Rit being the most popular brand. These dyes are concentrated, highly water-soluble, and have a wide range of color options. Simply follow the instructions on the packaging. Most require an additional fixative, like vinegar, for color fastness. If you're working with synthetic fabrics like polyester, seek out acid dyes made specifically for synthetics (Rit, Jacquard, and Dylon offer them).

**Fiber-reactive dyes:** These dyes are the best choice for cellulose fibers, like cotton, linen, rayon, hemp, bamboo, and silk. The dye result is superior because of the chemical bond itself, which becomes part of the fiber, rather than just staining the surface. Fiber-reactive dyes come in an array of beautiful colors, which are brilliant and permanent, and they tend not to fade, even after repeated washings. Follow the instructions on pages 200 and 201.

### Natural

**Natural dyes:** Colorants derived from plants, invertebrates, or minerals. See page 202 for tutorials and helpful information.

**Indigo dyes:** Natural indigo is an extract obtained through a nontoxic fermentation of the indigo plant. The traditional process for extracting the dye is very intensive, so I like working with indigo crystals, which dissolve in water and produce the same results. See page 204.

### Other Dyeing Tips

- If you are going to dye or paint any fabric before sewing, make sure to add at least 2 to 4 inches of additional length and width to your original cut, to account for shrinking and fraying that will occur during washing. Once you are done washing and ironing the fabric, cut out the measurement you need for your project.
- Don't be afraid to mix up your own colors. Try new combinations and methods. You never know what might strike your fancy or turn out to be just the perfect experiment. Just remember to keep notes. Jot down your ratios and processes so that you can achieve the same color at a later time.
- If you are not happy with the final results, you can always try using a reducing agent to remove the color. Look for dye remover from brands like Rit, Jacquard, and Dharma Trading Co.

# fiber-reactive dyeing

These are my favorite dyes to work with. They come in a vast array of beautiful colors and it's easy to blend colors to create your own shades. Fiber-reactive dyes work by using the addition of salt and soda ash, which helps the dye bind and adhere to the fabric permanently.

**SUPPLIES**

Gentle laundry detergent

1 pound dry, natural-fiber fabric (see Tips)

3 gallons warm water

3 to 6 tablespoons fiber-reactive dye in your desired color(s) (see Tips)

3 cups noniodized salt

1½ cups soda ash

**TOOLS**

Protective gear (rubber gloves, safety glasses, and face mask)

5-gallon bucket with lid

Measuring implements (spoons, cups, and pitchers)

Long wooden spoon or stirring stick

**1** Prewash your fabric with detergent to remove any grease, starch, or conditioners. Keep it damp, or wet the fabric before adding it to the dye. Put on your protective gear.

**2** Add the water to the bucket. To a small bowl, add the dye and pour in about a cup of lukewarm water. Stir to dissolve the dye, then pour it into the bucket.

**3** Stir in the noniodized salt and soda ash. (While some people swear by boiling the fabric in the soda ash solution before adding it to the dye, I don't find this necessary.)

**4** Add the damp fabric to the bucket. Using a long wooden spoon, stir gently and frequently for at least 15 minutes. Check the saturation. Once you achieve your desired shade, remove the fabric. For a deeper shade, you can leave it in for up to an hour.

**5** Rinse the fabric under cool water until the water runs clear. To help set the fabric, let it dry in the sun or place it in the dryer on the appropriate setting for the fabric. Before using, wash the fabric in the washing machine, by itself with detergent, then place it in the dryer on the appropriate setting.

**TIPS**

• This recipe works best for 1 pound of dry fabric, which can easily be weighed with a digital kitchen scale. Scale this recipe up or down based on your needs.

• The amount of dye you use will depend on the intensity of color you want (for a more intense shade, use more dye; for a paler shade, use less).

# ice-dyeing

Ice-dyeing is an easy technique using fiber-reactive dyes to make a colorful, almost crystallized pattern. As the ice melts over the fabric, it slowly disperses the dye and creates depth of color and multiple tones. Each dye session will yield stunning, one-of-a-kind results.

### SUPPLIES

Gentle laundry detergent

1 pound dry, natural-fiber fabric

3 gallons warm water

3 cups soda ash

5-pound bag of ice

1 tablespoon per color of fiber-reactive powder dye (see Tip)

### TOOLS

Protective gear (gloves, eye protection, and face mask)

5-gallon bucket

Measuring spoons

Plastic sheeting or drop cloth

Wide, plastic storage bin (like the kind used to store sweaters)

Large, wire cooling rack (big enough to span the top of the bin, or you can overlap 2 or more on top of the bin)

**1** Prewash your fabric with detergent to remove any grease, or conditioners. Put on your protective gear.

**2** Add the fabric and water to the bucket. Stir in the soda ash until it dissolves, then let the fabric soak for at least 15 minutes. Pull out the fabric and squeeze out the excess liquid.

**3** On a flat surface, place the plastic sheeting under the storage bin to protect the surface. Set the wire cooling rack on top of the bin.

**4** Scrunch up and twist the fabric loosely while placing it on top of the cooling rack. Make sure all the fabric stays within the edges of the plastic bin to keep any mess inside the bucket. Place a mound of ice on top of the fabric, covering as much of the fabric surface as possible.

**5** Using a spoon, sprinkle the dye on top of the ice, 1 color at a time. Try not to overlap colors too much or the finished color will look muddled. Allow the ice to melt completely and leave the fabric untouched for at least 12 hours and up to 24 hours.

**6** Carefully remove the fabric from the rack. Rinse the fabric under cool water until the water runs clear. To help set the fabric, let it dry in the sun or place it in the dryer on the appropriate setting for the fabric. Before using, wash the fabric in the washing machine, by itself with detergent, then place it in the dryer on the appropriate setting.

> **TIP**
> Use as many colors as you want. I've made beautiful fabric using 5 colors, but even 1 color will produce outstanding results.

# natural dyeing

Color can be coaxed from all kinds of natural sources, including plants, minerals, and invertebrates, which yield beautiful, exciting, and unexpected results. When working with natural dyes, it's important to remember that experimentation is key. Natural dyes work best with natural fibers like cotton, wool, silk, and linen (which better absorb the color). The color and saturation will vary depending on the amount of fruits or vegetables you use, how long you boil the product, or how long you leave the fibers in the dye. For long-lasting results, you might want to presoak your fabric in a color fixative made with water and salt (for berries) or vinegar (for other plants) before dyeing to help the color set in the fabric permanently. Not all dye materials need a fixative prior to dyeing, so it's best to test different variations in order to achieve the best result.

If you are using vegetation and plant material, go for fresh, ripe, and mature vegetation; stay away from anything dead or dried. Don't forget to look in your spice cabinet to get fabulous results, as we did with the Trimmed Waffle-Weave Blanket (page 122) dyed with turmeric powder.

SUPPLIES

½ cup salt (for fruit-based dyes), or 2 cups distilled white vinegar (for other plant- or vegetable-based dyes)

1 pound dry, natural-fiber fabric

2 cups or more berries, chopped vegetables, or other plants (see the Nature's Rainbow chart on the opposite page for color ideas from plant-based sources)

Woolite detergent or mild dish soap

TOOLS

Large stainless steel or other nonreactive pot

Protective gloves

Sieve or strainer

Stirring stick

**1** Place 8 cups of water and the salt or vinegar in the stainless steel pot. Submerge the fabric in the liquid and bring to a boil, then reduce to a simmer for an hour. Rinse the material under cool water until the water runs clear. Wearing gloves, squeeze out the excess liquid. Rinse the pot.

**2** Add the plant material to the pot with 16 cups of water. Bring to a boil, then reduce to a simmer for about an hour. Remove from the heat; strain out the solids and sediment, and return the colored liquid to the pot.

**3** Add the fabric to the dye pot and, over low heat, stir gently so that the fabric evenly absorbs the dye. If needed, you can add more water to the pot to cover the material. Leave the fabric in the dye solution until it reaches your desired saturation (the color will appear darker when wet and a bit lighter when dry). To ensure deeper color, let the material soak overnight.

**4** Rinse the fabric under cool water and hand-wash with Woolite detergent until the water runs clear. Hang to dry. Avoid machine washing and harsh detergents.

## NATURE'S RAINBOW

| If You're Going For... | Try These Ingredients... |
| --- | --- |
| Red | Beets, sumac, berries, huckleberries, pomegranate, bamboo, basil leaves, rose madder, bloodroot, alder, cranberries, birch |
| Pink | Raspberries, cherries, strawberries, red and pink roses, avocado skins and seeds |
| Orange | Carrots, gold lichen, onionskins, bloodroot, elm, blackberries |
| Yellow | Saffron, onionskins, turmeric, marigold, sunflower petals, dandelion flowers, paprika, celery leaves, yellow dock roots, St. John's wort |
| Green | Artichoke, spinach, peppermint leaves, grass, nettles, butterfly milkweed, stinging nettle |
| Blue | Indigo, red cabbage, dogwood bark, maple, elderberries, yellow iris roots |
| Purple | Blueberries, hairy coneflower, red bulberry, blackberries, plums, dandelion root |
| Brown | Prickly popply, elderberries, acorns, butternut squash, hazelnuts, oak, walnuts, onionskins |

# indigo dyeing

The procedure of setting up and maintaining an indigo vat is more complicated than you would expect, but it is intensely satisfying, as it yields an extraordinarily lovely color you'll want to keep for decades. When first starting out, dye a lot of test swatches so you can get a feel for the results while building up experience in all the various folds and dyeing techniques (see page 206). The possibilities are endless! Some companies, like Dharma Trading Co., sell an indigo tie-dye kit to streamline this process. But if you would like to start from scratch and learn the basics, gather the items listed below.

## SUPPLIES

One 50-gram bag prereduced indigo crystals

160 grams thiourea dioxide (also known as "thiox" and typically used as a color remover)

240 grams soda ash

1 pound dry, natural-fiber fabric

## TOOLS

Protective gear (gloves, eye protection, and organic vapor respirator)

Digital scale and small bowl, for measuring ingredients

5-gallon plastic bucket with lid (this will be called the "vat")

Long stirring stick or wooden spoon

Rubber bands, cotton twine, or clothespins (or other items for compressing and binding your cloth; see page 12 for more ideas)

Small plastic plate or container (for storing the "flower" before dyeing)

**1** If possible, work outdoors in a shady spot. Put on your protective gear. Make a vat with 4 gallons of lukewarm tap water. Add the indigo crystals and the thiourea dioxide to the vat and stir. Next, add the soda ash.

**2** Using a stirring stick, stir the ingredients in a circle, going in one direction only, for about 3 minutes. When stirring, try to keep excess air from getting into the liquid (as indigo reacts with oxygen). Slow down and reverse the direction of the stirring, dragging your stirring stick along the outer edge of the vat before removing the stirring stick. This will bring the foam that has formed, which is called the "flower," to the center of the vat. Let the mixture settle for at least an hour.

**3** Stir one more time and let the mixture sit for 15 minutes before dyeing your fabric. The liquid should be clear yellowish-green in color; a "flower" will sit on top as well as some coppery, metallic-looking film.

**4** Meanwhile, thoroughly soak the fabric in lukewarm water; squeeze out the excess. Fold the fabric, using any of the techniques on page 206, and secure with rubber bands, twine, or clothespins. Put on your protective gear.

**5** Skim the flower off the top of the liquid and set it aside on a plate. Push the fabric slowly into the vat, keeping it submerged for 30 seconds to 3 minutes. You don't want to stir up the sediment at the bottom of the vat; that might create unwanted dark spots in your final product.

**6** Squeeze the fabric as you lift it out, trying not to drip or make bubbles. When you lift the fabric out, it will be a yellow-green color. Now, this is where the magic happens. As the air hits the fabric, the indigo will gradually oxidize and the fabric will turn a brilliant blue. Let the fabric oxidize for approximately 15 minutes.

**7** If desired, you can re-dip your fabric to achieve a darker shade. After each oxidation, repeat dipping into the indigo vat for 30 seconds to 3 minutes, and let it oxidize until you've reached the desired depth of blue. Keep in mind that, after washing the fabric, the final color will be one to two shades lighter. When you are satisfied with the color, rinse and untie the fabric, then wash it separately according to the fabric content.

**8** When you are finished dyeing, put the flower back into the vat and stir the vat in the same circular manner as described in step 2. Put the lid on the vat and store at room temperature until your next dye session. The indigo vat will last for several weeks or months with continued use.

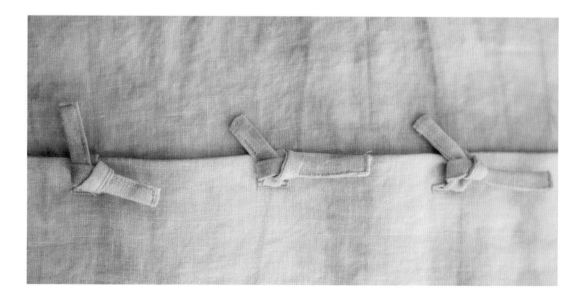

## FOLDING FABRIC TO CREATE PATTERNS

Shibori is a Japanese dyeing technique that involves folding, compressing, twisting, or bunching cloth and binding it before adding it to a dye bath. Whatever you use to bind the fabric will resist the dye and remain white, resulting in patterns. There are myriad ways to create shibori patterns. Here are a few used throughout the book:

**Arashi (pole wrap):** This scrunched fold results in a long, and often thin, striped pattern. Create it by wrapping the width of the fabric around a pole, such as a PVC pipe, and secure it by tying a piece of twine to one end of the pole then winding the twine around the fabric several times until you reach the other end of the pole. Scrunch the fabric down into folds (to create tight crinkles) and dip the pole with the fabric into the dye.

**Itajime (shaped resist):** This pattern creates large areas of negative space, with the most popular pattern made using an accordion fold. Lay fabric on a flat surface. Fold the fabric into even sections lengthwise, reversing the direction at each fold, like an accordion, to get a skinny rectangle. Then fold the length of the rectangle, using the same method, to get a tight square. Place the final piece between two pieces of wood, then bind everything together with string, rubber bands, or clamps.

**Kanoko (bound resist):** Traditionally thought of as tie-dye, this technique is done by tying the fabric in areas where you would like the dye to be resisted. You can do this any number of ways and using various objects to achieve the desired effect of the resist. Variations include bunching small sections of the fabric and securing with rubber bands, twisting all of the fabric randomly and clamping it, or folding it into shapes and binding with twine.

# sewing

It is good to have some basic sewing terminology in your DIY vocabulary. Most of the sewing projects in this book reference the following techniques and terminology. When in doubt, I like to Google Image a stitch name or sewing term for up close and personal thread pictures. (Seriously, what did we do before the Internet?) Also, before you get all bogged down in the words, take a moment to sit with your project and just think about how you would do it. Thinking about the construction beforehand will help you avoid making mistakes. Lastly, remember to measure twice and cut once.

**Anchor machine stitch:** Place the needle into the fabric where you want to begin a seam. Make three stitches, then reverse direction and make two stitches. Switch back to go forward and complete the length of your seam.

**Double-fold hem:** Place fabric, right side down, on a flat surface. Using the required hem allowance specified in the project, measure and mark the hem allowance from the raw edge of the fabric, then fold the edge over to the mark so

that the wrong sides are touching. Iron this single fold flat. Make a second fold by tucking the raw edge underneath the single fold so that the raw edge meets the fold and creates a double hem (the raw edge is no longer visible). Secure this double fold with pins for easier sewing of the seam. Sew a straight stitch by hand or with a sewing machine close to the fabric's edge (or at the measurement specified in the project).

**French seams:** When sewing two pieces together, especially linen fabric, French seams work really well because they enclose all the raw edges, which tend to unravel with linen. Plus, they look really nice. To make French seams, match up the right sides of the two pieces of fabric on a flat surface. Pin one edge of the two layers together to secure before sewing. Stitch the seam using the required seam measurement. Trim away all but the seam allowance specified in the project. Once the two layers are trimmed, fold the fabric edges at the seam back onto themselves; iron and secure with pins. Sew a ½-inch seam using the required seam allowance (or the amount specified in the project). Iron the seam.

**Hem:** The raw edge of fabric that has been turned under and sewn.

**Interfacing:** A moderately stiff fabric used between the inner and outer layers to enhance the strength or shape of a piece.

**Notched corners (or mitered corners):** To achieve smooth, flat corners and curves (especially when making pillows), it is helpful to clip some of the fabric along the seam allowance of the corner or curve so that the fabric doesn't bulk up. Do this after you've sewn two pieces of fabric together; turn the pieces inside out and clip off the corners. If working with a curve in the seam, then clip out notches or Vs into the seam allowance.

**Raw edge of fabric:** The outside edge of the fabric that has not been sewn in any way. The raw edge includes both the selvage and the cut edge.

**Right side of fabric:** The "right" side of the fabric is the printed side.

**Running stitch:** A simple needlework stitch consisting of a line of small, even stitches that run in and out throughout the cloth without overlapping.

**Seam:** The stitching that holds two or more pieces together.

**Seam allowance:** The measurement between the edge of the fabric and the stitching line.

**Slip stitch:** A hand-sewing technique also known as a blind stitch or an invisible stitch used to close up a hole after turning your fabric right side out, such as when you're finishing a pillow. Add a few pins to line up the top edges of the folds and secure the hole. Thread a sewing needle with 18 inches of thread. Knot one end of the thread. Beginning on one end of the hole, insert your needle into the inside fold of the hem, then push the needle through to catch a few threads of the opposite fold (without going through the outside of the fabric), then back into the folded hem for the next stitch. Repeat this back and forth stitching down the entire length of the hole. When you get to the end of the hole, tie off your thread to the fabric inside the fold; trim the tail with scissors.

**Wrong side of fabric:** The "wrong" side of the fabric is the side you don't see once your project is completed.

# woodworking

Here is a basic overview of the important techniques called for in my wood projects. As with sewing, make sure to measure twice, cut once.

## How to Drill a Hole

Learn these easy tricks to help you drill a superior hole. Make sure to have a good electric drill on hand for this task—a little extra power goes a long way!

**Basic hole:** Always mark with a pencil exactly where the hole needs to go. It works best if you make an indentation in the wood to help catch the drill bit in the right place. Load your drill with the appropriately sized drill bit. Turn the drill to the side slightly to line up the very tip of the drill bit with the indentation you made in the wood. Then turn the drill bit up at a 90-degree angle, perpendicular to the object you are drilling. Start slowly, so the drill bit doesn't jump. Once you've created a small hole, push down firmly on the drill until you feel less resistance, which usually means you've gone through the object successfully. When you are drilling a large hole, take it slow. You can move the drill bit up and down to help remove the debris that is being created.

This will clear the way down. When you've finished drilling the hole, keep the drill rotating at a slow speed and pull it back out. Blow away the dust; sand the hole, if necessary; and you're done.

**Measured depth trick:** Use painter's tape to mark how deep you want to drill into the wood. If you need to drill only a ½-inch-deep hole, measure from the tip of the drill bit and place a piece of tape right at the end of the ½-inch mark on the bit. Put the tape on like a little flag: center the middle and wrap the two ends around to meet and stick together. As you are drilling, stop when you get to the tape.

**Pilot hole:** Sometimes it is best to drill a pilot hole first. This is a small hole that will help guide a larger drill bit down in the right place.

## How to Cut Wood

The easiest way to cut wood for big projects like furniture is with an electric saw blade, rather than a handsaw (though you can certainly use a handsaw). What you want to remember when marking wood before cutting it is that the saw blade has a width that you'll need to take into account when measuring for the cut. The width of the saw blade will disappear from the wood, so always mark your measurement with a pencil line, then know which side of the line to cut. You can do this by placing an X or an arrow on the correct side as a reminder. When making identical cuts, measure the next piece from the fresh cut to ensure that all the cut pieces will match up.

To make a clean cut and to prevent injuries, always brace or support the wood you are about to cut. Set up a big enough work space to hold the length of the wood up to the cutting line, so you can support the wood using your free hand or with the help of a clamp or a vise.

### How to Cut a Miter Joint

A miter joint is made by angling two pieces of wood, usually at a 45-degree angle, so they form a corner when joined together. Most picture frames are made by combining four miter joints. Miter joints are most accurate when cut by a machine. But you can accurately cut them by hand with a little patience and practice. With an electric miter box, you can lock the saw in at the 45-degree mark and cut. Same goes for a miter box, which is an inexpensive gadget that holds your wood and the saw at a specific angle while you saw the wood by hand. Remember to cut to the outside of the marked line, or you run the risk that the joints won't match up evenly. Don't forget to reverse your angle on the other end of the wood if you need

two miter joints, as you do when making a frame.

If you are a beginner, it is best to cut your angles a tad longer because you can always remove more wood. Try to keep the saw blade completely straight as you cut. It is difficult to get two uneven cuts to match up perfectly; any glue will be exposed and your finished piece will look messy. When joining two miter cuts with various fasteners, like nails, it is always a good idea to also add wood glue.

### How to Apply Wood Glue

To successfully glue one board to another, follow these simple steps. Purchase regular wood glue, such as Elmer's Carpenter's Wood Glue or Titebond Wood Glue, which are my favorites. Make sure the surfaces to be glued are smooth, dry, and free of dirt and dust. You can apply the glue most accurately to small spaces using a cheap paintbrush. For larger areas, you can use the bottle to apply the glue directly to the board. Apply the glue to both mating surfaces, spreading it evenly with a paintbrush or spreader. Push the glued pieces together and give them a little rub back and forth to help even out the glue for a successful join. Once the pieces are lined up, use clamps to hold them in place until the glue fully cures. When you clamp boards together, sometimes glue will seep out. Simply wipe it clean with a paper towel. You can scrape off any dried glue with a sander or chisel once the boards are ready to come out of the clamps.

# leather cutting

Leather strips are often sold in precut lengths, called straps, but they're not always the width you need. You can easily cut straight leather strips by hand with a little bit of effort and with tools you may already have on hand.

## SUPPLIES
Leather hide, at least as wide in 1 direction as the length you need

## TOOLS
Cutting mat

Quilter's ruler, 24 to 36 inches long (a quilter's square ruler is also helpful if your leather doesn't lie completely flat)

60 mm rotary cutter (the sharper the blade, the better)

Pencil

**1** Lay the leather down flat on the cutting mat. Figure out the width and thickness of the strips you will be cutting (see Tips).

**2** Line up your ruler for the first cut, preferably from one end of the hide to the other for the most economical use.

**3** Press down firmly on the ruler while it is resting on the leather to keep both the ruler and the leather from slipping while you cut. Start at the bottom of the ruler, closest to you, and firmly roll the blade over the leather, staying right at the ruler's edge. Be careful not to move the ruler out of position. Cut 1 solid line and repeat in the opposite direction if the blade didn't go through the entire thickness of the leather. If you are working with a larger hide you can cut the entire length of the ruler, then drag it up to match your line and continue cutting the remaining width.

**4** Make a couple of pencil marks indicating where the next cut should go. Position your ruler to make the second cut and complete the first strip. It is important for the ruler to stay an equal distance away from your first cut along the entire length; otherwise, you will end up with an uneven strip. Also, keep in mind that the blade has a thickness and you should cut right on the marked line or right outside of it to prevent lost thickness.

**5** Continue moving across the leather, cutting as many strips as you need. To square the ends, use a ruler or a square ruler to cut off the uneven ends.

**TIPS**

• If you plan to cut a lot of leather strips, it might be worth investing in a strap cutter, a hand tool that easily and efficiently cuts even strips (usually up to 4 inches wide).

• Never iron leather, use straight pins on leather, or get leather wet, unless you are shape-forming or work-hardening the leather.

# mirror antiquing

I love the look of an antique mirror. You can add vintage appeal and character to almost any mirror with some basic supplies from your local hardware store. Try this technique on large or small mirrors. While this is a great skill, it isn't a quick process; it's also messy and requires serious attention to safety. You will be highly rewarded for your efforts, though—a distressed mirror never goes out of style!

**SUPPLIES**

Mirror

Citri-Strip Safer Paint and Varnish Stripping Gel (see Tip)

Mineral spirits

Cheesecloth

Bleach (see Tip)

Can of spray paint in black or any color of your choosing

Can of Krylon Looking Glass Spray Paint (optional)

Glass cleaner

**TOOLS**

Thick plastic drop cloths

Protective gear (chemical-resistant gloves, safety glasses, and vapor respirator)

2 to 3-inch cheap or old paintbrush

Paint scraper

Plastic garbage bag

Fine-mist spray bottle

**TIP**

The chemicals used to strip away the mirror backing should be used with caution. Make sure to wear your safety gear and, if possible, work outdoors or in a well-ventilated area. Keep away from children and pets.

**1** Prepare your work surface: Place a layer or 2 of thick plastic drop cloths down to protect your work area. Position the mirror with the back facing up in the center of the drop cloth. (You can do more than one mirror at a time.)

**2** Put on your safety gear. To strip the mirror backing, pour enough stripper on the mirror back to evenly coat the surface. Spread the stripper around evenly, using the paintbrush to get a nice thick layer. (Don't bother cleaning your brush after this; just discard it when you're done.) Leave the stripper on for at least 12 hours and up to 24 hours (you'll know the process is finished when you see small bubbles all along the outer edge).

**3** Use the scraper to gently remove the gray and copper layers of the mirror backing. You should see a nice, shiny gold or silver layer hiding under all the goop. Scrape all the goop to the sides and toss it in a plastic bag to discard. Keep in mind that this is toxic and should be disposed of properly.

**4** Using mineral spirits, clean off all the leftover chemical residue with a soft material like cheesecloth. Be very careful not to scratch the mirror surface.

**5** Carefully pour some bleach into a fine-mist spray bottle. Spray the mirror backing with small squirts of the bleach. Wherever you choose to spray, the bleach will remove the mirror finish, so just spray the edges or try for a few spots in the middle of the mirror. Don't go overboard or you risk erasing the entire mirrored surface and ending up with nothing but a clear piece of glass. The bleach works really fast. Just spray a little at a time until you work up to the level of removal you want. Let it sit for an hour to dry completely.

**6** Bring the mirror over to a sink, if the mirror is small enough, and rinse off all the bleach. If you are working with a large mirror, use a hose or a soft rag soaked in water to wash off the surface. Remember that the bleach is still active and will bleach anything it comes in contact with, so be careful. Once the mirror is clean, let it dry completely before moving on to the next step.

**7** In order to antique the mirror and protect the back from scratching, you need to spray the back with spray paint, which will fill in the holes you made with the bleach. I like to layer color and an additional faux-mirror spray paint. The look of the two combined gives the mirror a little more depth (as shown below). You can also just spray an even layer of 1 color onto the back, if you like. Spray a couple coats of paint, allowing each coat to dry between painting sessions.

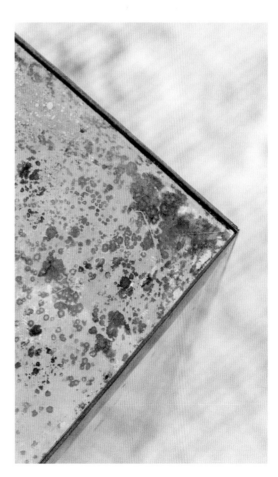

# resources

One of the hardest parts about starting a new project is not knowing where to find the right materials. If an item on a project supply list was purchased from a specific company, I have listed it for you in the tutorial. Hopefully, this will help cut out some legwork and get you started in the right place. Following is a list of terrific art suppliers and brands that I use and trust. Don't be afraid to deviate from the items listed below and in each tutorial; there are so many wonderful companies out there making great things.

### General Craft Materials

A.C. Moore Arts & Crafts
www.acmoore.com

Artist & Craftsman Supply
www.artistcraftsman.com

Dick Blick Art Materials
www.dickblick.com

Jamali Floral & Garden Supplies
www.jamaligarden.com

Shipwreck Beads
www.shipwreckbeads.com

Uline
www.uline.com

### Dyes, Paint, and Art Supplies

Aurora Silk
www.aurorasilk.com

Dharma Trading Co.
www.dharmatrading.com

Jacquard
www.jacquardproducts.com

Montana-Cans
www.montana-cans.com

Pébéo
www.pebeo.com

The Rit Studio
www.ritstudio.com

### Fabric and Notions

B&J Fabrics
www.bandjfabrics.com

Fabric.com
www.fabric.com

Fabrics-Store.com
www.fabrics-store.com

Fashion Fabrics Club
www.fashionfabricsclub.com

Jo-Ann Fabric and Craft Stores
www.joann.com

Liberty London
www.libertylondon.com

M&J Trimming
www.mjtrim.com

Online Fabric Store
www.onlinefabricstore.net

Organic Cotton Plus
www.organiccottonplus.com

Purl Soho
www.purlsoho.com

Spoonflower
www.spoonflower.com

Webs
www.yarn.com

## Leather and Leather Tools

Leather Cord USA
www.leathercordusa.com

Leather Impact
www.leatherimpact.com

Tandy Leather
www.tandyleather.com

Zack White Leather Co.
www.zackwhite.com

## Hardware, Tools, and Wood

Casey's Wood Products
www.caseyswood.com

DIY Upholstery Supply LLC
www.diyupholsterysupply.com

Hairpinlegs.com
www.hairpinlegs.com

The Home Depot
www.homedepot.com

Lowe's
www.lowes.com

TableLegs.com
www.tablelegs.com

Van Dyke's Restorers
www.vandykes.com

Woodworks Ltd.
www.craftparts.com

## Electrical and Lighting Supply

Color Cord Company
www.colorcord.com

The Lamp Shop
www.lampshop.com

Sundial Wire
www.sundialwire.com

## Alternative Materials

Canal Plastics Center
www.canalplastic.com

Crystal River Gems
www.crystalrivergems.com

TAP Plastics
www.tapplastics.com

T&T PlasticLand
www.ttplasticland.com

## Reuse and Thrift Stores

Big Reuse
www.bigreuse.org

Craigslist
www.craigslist.com

Habitat for Humanity ReStore
www.habitat.org/restores

The ReUse Warehouse
www.thereusewarehouse.com

The Scrap Exchange
www.scrapexchange.org

# acknowledgments

To my best friend and husband, Collin. Thank you for not only being involved but also being interested in my many endeavors. Your unwavering enthusiasm for life and learning is infectious. I love you. Home is wherever you are.

A huge, gigantic, forever and always thank-you to my parents. Mom, Dad, this book wouldn't have seen the light of day without your support, encouragement, and hard work. Thank you for teaching me how to make things! Also, thank you for taking such good care of Davie anytime I needed you to, and for putting in long hours with me to help me finish all these projects. You both raise the bar on what it means to love. I love you tremendously.

To Pat and Jack—I truly did win the in-law lottery. Thank you for all your support and enthusiasm, which typically translate into heavy lifting and baby duty. You are always there for us and I love you.

To my lovely editor, Angelin Borsics, thank you for championing my dream book and for making me sound like a million bucks. You brought out the best of my vision and made it truly beautiful. Thank you also for that coffee stain on my edits; it made me smile.

This book simply would not have been possible without the wonderful team at Penguin Random House/Clarkson Potter, specifically Debbie Glasserman, Patricia Shaw, and Kevin Garcia. Thank you all for your endless enthusiasm, attention to detail, and guidance.

To Julia Wade, who rocked the socks off these photographs. This project shines because of your insane talent. Thank you for your positivity, friendship, and very large minivan— and for owning the process from day one.

A heartfelt thank-you to Tate Obayashi, who drew the sweetest illustrations for this book. You have been a wonderful friend and huge help to me through many years and I am so very thankful for you.

To Lisa Tauber, who saw my vision and gave it a chance. Thank you immensely for your vote of confidence. I hope I made you proud.

A big thank-you to Shelly, Emily, Arielle, Meghan, and Tate for helping me to get this book started in the right direction. I miss my dream team.

Pat, thank you for letting me prop-shop your house and for trusting me with your beautiful books and artwork.

Thank you to the wonderful team at Nomadic Trading Co. (www.nomadictrading.com), for letting me search endlessly through the insanely beautiful piles of rugs and then trusting me to cart them all over town. They made the rooms pop!

To all the homeowners who graciously welcomed me and all my projects into your homes for this book, I am so grateful: Lisa and Justin Hauenstein (www.threeinteriors.com), Steven Burke and Randy Campbell (www.americanfolkartbuildings.org), and Rachel and Joseph Bradley (www.josephbradleystudio.com). This book comes to life because of the love, care, and personality that you put into your living spaces. Thank you!

Lastly, to my sweet Davie, I love you. You are my wish.

# index